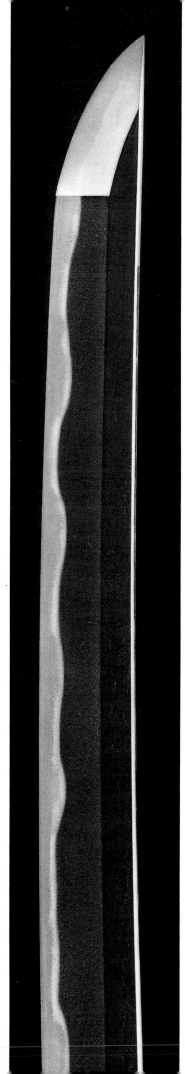

SWORDS
OF THE
SAMURAI

SWORDS
OF THE
SAMURAI

VICTOR HARRIS
AND NOBUO OGASAWARA

Published for the Trustees of the British Museum
by British Museum Publications

© 1990 The Trustees of the British Museum

Published by British Museum Publications Ltd
46 Bloomsbury Street, London WC1B 3QQ

British Library Cataloguing in Publication Data

Harris, Victor
    Swords of the Samurai.
    1. Japan. Samurai, history
    I. Title II. Ogasawara, Nobuo
    305.52

    ISBN 0–7141–1450–2

Designed by Harry Green

Set in Palatino and printed in Great Britain by
Butler & Tanner Ltd, Frome and London

Page 1 Katana blade (no. 55), Momoyama period,
c. 1610; Tadayoshi.

Pages 2–3 Detail of tsuba (no. 124), Edo period, 18th–
19th century; Masatsune.

Cover Katana blade (no. 75), Edo period, 17th century;
Sukenao. (British Museum.)

Detail from a six-fold screen, showing the battles of
Yashima and Ichinotani, Edo period, 17th century.
(British Museum.)

The Trustees of the British Museum acknowledge
with gratitude generous assistance towards the
production of this book from the
Token Kai of Great Britain,
the Society for the Study and Preservation of
Japanese Swords in the United Kingdom and Europe

Contents

Message

from Nakae Toshitada, President, Asahi Shimbun

It is a great pleasure for me that the Asahi Shimbun has been instrumental in bringing about this first loan exhibition from Japan of Japanese swords to the new Japanese Gallery at the British Museum. It was following the opening of the loan exhibition of Ukiyoe art from the British Museum's collection in Tokyo in 1985 that Sir David Wilson, the Director, formerly requested the continuing co-operation of the Asahi Shimbun in order to build the new Japanese Gallery. At the time it was agreed that a number of exhibitions should be held in Japan as part of the programme of co-operation, starting with *Masterpieces of Chinese and Japanese Art in the British Museum* which was held at four major cities in 1987. In continuation, *Treasures of the British Museum* will tour Tokyo, Yamaguchi and Osaka between October 1990 and May 1991. It is a great honour to me that the Asahi Shimbun has been able to co-operate in this way towards the promotion of cultural exchange between Japan and England.

This exhibition, *Swords of the Samurai*, will introduce the unique art form of the finely polished Japanese sword, showing the development from the ancient straight blades introduced from China and Korea to the finally perfected curved Japanese sword. It is my special hope that the many people who visit the gallery will understand and enjoy this highly spiritual aspect of Japanese culture.

Finally I should like to thank the sword specialists who planned this exhibition – Victor Harris of the British Museum and his friend Nobulo Ogasawara, Keeper of Swords at the Tokyo National Museum, who spared no efforts in his support – the personnel of the Society for the Preservation of Japanese Art Swords, the Agency for Cultural Affairs of the Japanese Government, the many owners of the exhibits, and those institutions who have provided financial assistance, having recognised the value of such an exhibition – the Toshiba International Foundation and Japan Airlines – together with all other persons who have helped in some way.

Message

from David M. Wilson, Director, British Museum

It is appropriate that this, the first of a series of major loan exhibitions from Japan arranged with the support of the Asahi Shimbun, should be of Japanese swords. The sword has been the major weapon of almost every culture throughout history and is a sure indication of the level of technology achieved in each period. This is particularly true of Japan, where swords made over 1,000 years ago demonstrate an extraordinary understanding of the metallurgy of steel which one cannot resist comparing with the achievements of recent Japanese technology.

The Japanese sword is one of the most striking artefacts to be found in Western collections of Japanese antiquities, and although it is central to a certain popular and semi-mythical image of Japanese society throughout history, its proper study has remained comparatively neglected. It is hoped that this exhibition, which includes examples of the most important schools of swordmaking from the ninth century onwards, will show clearly the importance of the sword in its relation to Japanese history and clarify the varying role of the samurai class through the social and political changes up to its abolition in 1876.

The Trustees of the British Museum are most grateful to the Asahi Shimbun for sponsoring this loan, and to the Agency for Cultural Affairs of the Japanese Government, the Toshiba International Foundation and Japan Airlines for their support. On their behalf I would particularly wish to thank the Director and staff of the Tokyo National Museum, the Kyoto National Museum, Kanagawa Prefectural Museum, the Swords Museum and members of the Society for the Preservation of Japan Art Swords for their goodwill in lending the material which has made this exhibition possible.

Acknowledgements

Thanks are due to a great number of people who have contributed either directly or indirectly with material help or by supporting, both in Japan and in the United Kingdom, the concept of the exhibition. The Director of the Tokyo National Museum kindly agreed to provide the major part of the loan, which was selected together with my dear colleague Nobuo Ogasawara, Keeper of Swords in that Museum, to whom I am also grateful for his kind guidance over the years. Other colleagues and friends in Kanagawa Prefectural Museum, Kazuhiko Inada of the Kyoto National Museum, Yuichi Hiroi of the Agency of Cultural Affairs, and the Society for the Preservation of Japan Art Swords have been no less helpful in many ways. Many people have contributed valuable and important material from their own collections, including Yoneyama Takamichi, Koike Shōnosuke, Kamijō Kiyoshi, Ōtsuki Kōchi, Ishikura Tsuneo, Kawabata Terutaka, Ishizuka Takao, Fukuoka Tatsuki, Otsuka Genichi, Itō Seisuke, Kanie Eikichi, Sugimoto Yoshimi, Fukazawa Toshihiko, Kishida Eisaku, Sasano Taikō, Abe Keigo, Miyake Teruyoshi, Shindō Tetsuo, Wakayama Takeshi, Fukushi Shigeo, Nobuo Ogasawara, Inakazu Daizō, Sumi Kenji, Tanobe Michihiro, Satō Yuriko, Takahashi Toshio, Shimano Kunio, Ōya Sadao, Yoshikawa Mutsuko and Takeda Masahiko.

The President and members of staff of the Asahi Shimbun, without whom this exhibition would not have been possible, have shown unfailing support and friendship. Members the Department of Japanese Antiquities have patiently tolerated my absences from the hard exhibition programme while this catalogue was being prepared. I am especially grateful to both Mr Hisama Ryuichi of Ōtsuka Kogeisha and the Swords Museum who freely lent many of the photographs for the book.

Finally I should like to thank Fred Stride, scientist and connoisseur, for reading the draft text, the designer Harry Green for applying his creative flair, and Deborah Wakeling for her patient and painstaking editing of a text which was presented to her at an unreasonably late date.

The inspiration for this exhibition was born twenty years ago during my period of study in Tokyo, when I had the fortune to be introduced by the late Dr Itō Kyoitsu to the late Dr Satō Kanzan of the Swords Museum, who instilled in me a sound basis for the study of the Japanese sword.

VICTOR HARRIS
Japanese Antiquities, British Museum

Preface

In no other culture has the sword been developed to such a level of technological excellence, and attained such a position of spiritual importance, as in Japan. As a cutting weapon the fully developed curved sword of the samurai is extremely effective. It is called upon to remain sharp even when used to cut through armour, and yet not to bend or break in use. Complex traditional methods of forging, conducted according to the ancient precepts of reverence and cleanliness of the Shintō religion, impart these qualities. Countless varying hues and patterns of the crystalline structures of steel which result from special methods of forging and heat treating are visible on the surface of a finely polished blade. In these textures lies an extraordinary and unique feature of the sword of the samurai – the steel itself possesses an intrinsic beauty not found on any other artefact of any culture. Moreover, just as a ceramic might be valued both for its surface texture and its form, the samurai sword is admired also for its elegant curve and crisply finished lines.

The Japanese sword has been appreciated as an art object since its perfection some time during the tenth century AD. Fine swords have been more highly prized than lands and riches, those of superior quality being handed down from generation to generation. In fact, many well-documented swords, whose blades are signed by their makers, survive from nearly 1,000 years ago. Recognisable features of the blades of hundreds of schools of swordmaking have been recorded punctiliously over the ages. The curve and proportions of the single-edged sword noticeably changed over the centuries against clearly definable social and geographical backgrounds. Since generally Japanese swords are inscribed with the name of the smith, and very often his place of work, title and the date of manufacture, the study of the sword is a certain guide to the flow of Japanese history.

Together with the mirror and jewel the sword forms part of the Imperial regalia of Japan. It has always been considered to contain a spiritual quality of its own: in shrines of the Shintō religion even today blades made 1,000 years ago are revered as the very manifestation of one of the *kami*, or gods of the Shintō religion. But ultimately the sword meant more to the samurai, for *kendō*, or sword fencing, in addition to being a military art was the means of a samurai's moral education, and the way leading to spiritual advancement. Zen Buddhism nurtured the concept of living and dying according to the precepts of swordsmanship, and the sword came to be considered an instrument of enlightenment.

This exhibition attempts to follow all aspects of the sword in Japanese culture from the first introduction of iron blades from China in the Yayoi period, some time around the beginning or just before the Christian era. Swords of the finest quality are shown from each of the main periods, together with their mountings, armour worn by the samurai, as well as contemporary paintings and other documents.

The Japanese sword – an appreciation

Nobuo Ogasawara

Every country in the world has a long history of swords and sword decoration. The longing for a superior weapon has given birth to countless myths and legends. But the custom of richly ornamenting the sword arises from reasons deeper than simply pride in possession. An ornate sword is not just a personal accessory, like rich clothing reflecting one's social position; it invariably has a deeper spiritual significance. In Japan the embellishing of swords with precious metals and jewels has always been more frugal than in other countries of Asia and Europe. However, in place of rich mountings a polishing process was developed which allowed an appreciation of the beauty in the grain of the steel, and in the *hamon*, the crystalline patterns along the hardened edge of the blade. This appreciation of beauty transcends the mere function of the sword as a weapon, and the Japanese sword blade has traditionally been considered as a work of art in its own right. For this reason a high level of technology was developed to mix different kinds of steels together in order to present aesthetic variations in the hamon and patterns on the surface of the blade.

Japanese culture grew in the past with cultural input from China and the Korean peninsula in all fields, including swords. The use of such expressions as *kara tachi* ('Chinese swords'), and *koma tsurugi* ('Korean swords') in the eighth century implies that Japanese fashion and technology were then inferior to that of the continent. However, there were poems extolling the splendour of Japanese swords in China during the Song dynasty, so Japanese technology must by then have far outpassed that of China. In the same way that Japan, as an island separated from the Asian continent, digested the religions and philosophy of Buddhism and Confucianism, and developed them further in its own special way, so the unique world of the Japanese sword was born. Although it has not yet been satisfactorily resolved whether the transformation of the ancient straight blade into the curved sword happened in Japan or whether it evolved from abroad, it is certain that the custom of wielding the long curved sword with a *shinogi* (longitudinal line separating the parallel section of the blade from the angled section which forms the cutting edge) in both hands is essentially Japanese.

The position of the sword as a work of art has raised some controversy even in Japan. Extremists claim that the sword is nothing more than an implement, and insist that 'art' be limited to paintings, sculpture and such; but it cannot be denied that the sword has an intrinsic beauty. All implements have a function to fulfil, without which they are useless, and all implements can possess a beauty of their own. Many people instinctively dislike the sword because of its original function, just as many people dislike wine because it can cause drunkenness; but both these attitudes ignore excellence because of narrow preconceptions.

In the diary of a sixteenth-century Portuguese missionary, Valignano, we read:

> Since excellent swords are valued in all countries it might be thought natural that the Japanese should open their hearts to these weapons, but they are excessive in this respect. Why, they pay so much as three, four, or five thousand ducats for one sword! I have myself seen several such valuable swords. The Lord of Bungo showed me one which he had bought for five thousand ducats. But the guard was not even of gold – it was nothing more than plain iron. When I asked him why he paid such prices for things of no value, he replied that it was for the same reason that we spend such sums on diamonds and rubies.

Although the present attitude to the Japanese sword might have changed somewhat, it would not be unnatural to hear the same words said today. The value of the sword lies to a great extent in the saying 'The sword is the soul of the *bushi*'. Here the word 'soul' (*kokoro* in Japanese) contains something of the meaning of heart, spirit and symbol. The *bushi*, the warrior class of Japan, originated as the guards of the estates of the nobility around the ninth century, eventually becoming respected members of society and acquiring their own political power. As times changed so did ideas. More recently, in the seventeenth century, the ideology of Confucianism became deeply permeated throughout Japanese society, bringing concepts of loyalty to one's lord, filial piety, personal humility and the readiness to die in an instant in the cause of justice. The idealised bushi was considered the perfect human being. For the Japanese people all this is symbolised by the sword.

What, then, is this beauty in the blade of the Japanese sword? It has been recognised since the distant past in

books listing the names of swordsmiths and the style and
characteristics of their blades, one of which exists from
the Kamakura period (thirteenth to fourteenth centuries).
We know that there were specialist appraisers in those
days, and there are records of the vocabulary used to
describe blade characteristics and the delicate changes in
texture revealed in the surface of a skilfully polished blade.
We can see today the very same swords, some of which
have been carefully preserved in perfect condition for
1,000 years. Perhaps the appreciation of swords is
something which derives from the artistic sense of the
Japanese, for it is certainly intimately connected with the
spiritual basis of Japanese culture – Zen, the Nō theatre,
the Tea Ceremony immediately spring to mind. But the
spirit of the bushi is a necessary basis for the understanding
of all these arts: it is the underlying concept of Michi
('The Way'), which is of such importance in arts such as
kyūdō (archery), where the object is more than just hitting
the target, and *kendō* (swordplay), in which the object is
more than just beating the opponent.

Even though the blade has been treasured since the
distant past, fashions in sword-mountings have changed
through the ages, and not many old mountings survive.
Although the form of ceremonial swords used at court
by both the aristocracy and the military remained
unchanged for several hundred years, there have been
great changes in the mountings of swords for general use.
The greatest change was during the sixteenth century,
when the custom of hanging tachi-type swords from the
belt gave way to the uchigatana, which was carried thrust
through the belt. The metal fittings on the uchigatana –
the tsuba, kozuka, menuki, and so on – in time became
decorative accessories. The designs on these pieces reflect
contemporary fashions, and many illustrate stories
indicating the education of the bushi. Perhaps there is
something superficial about the decoration of sword-
fittings, but the technical level of the metalwork is very
high, and this alone invites a special kind of appreciation.

I believe that this exhibition, *Swords of the Samurai*, the
first of a series of loan exhibitions from Japan in the new
Japanese Gallery at the British Museum, reflects and
confirms an existing understanding of the saying 'The
sword is the soul of the bushi'. The Japanese sword, with
its innate spiritual quality, is an incomparable work of art.

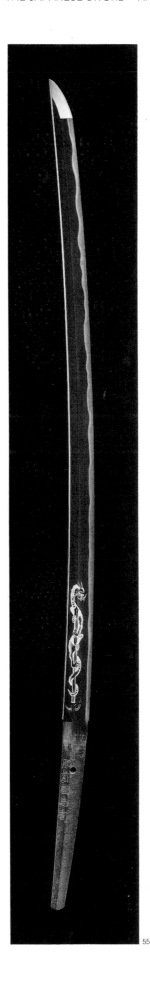

55

Introduction

The manufacture of the blade

The requirements of a sword, that it will maintain a sharp edge and will neither bend nor break during combat, are obtained from a forging process whereby the steel is repeatedly folded to give it strength, and a separate process of heat treating the edge to harden it. The grain formed by the folding, and a crystalline structure along the cutting edge which results from the final hardening process, are found first on the *chokutō*, or straight swords, which originated in China and have been excavated from tombs of the Kofun period (*c.* third to sixth centuries AD) in Japan.

The original Chinese technology was taken and improved upon, the method of manufacture becoming increasingly sophisticated, until around the middle of the Heian period (794–1185) steels of differing quality were combined to give improved mechanical qualities. While there are several methods of combining such steels, basically most depend upon a longitudinal inner core of soft and resilient steel, or *shingane*, and an outer skin of much harder steel, or *hadagane*. The steels are prepared by a process of continually heating the billet until it is malleable, beating it out into an oblong, then folding and welding the folded halves together. The smith uses steel refined from iron ore using charcoal. The degree of purity and carbon content are adjusted both before the process of forging and during it. This folding process might be repeated just a few times for the shingane and perhaps a dozen times for the hadagane, thus producing a characteristic grain visible in the finally polished blade.

The hardened edge is made by first coating the blade with a mixture of clays and ashes and partially scraping this off along the edge. The blade is then heated, traditionally to the colour of the moon in February or August. It is next quenched in a trough of cold water, which results in a largely pearlitic structure on the body and the hard martensitic structure of tool steel along the edge. The hard edge maintains extreme sharpness, and the more resilient body and soft shingane provide the robustness needed to bear the impacts of combat. The hard crystalline structure running along the length of the blade a few millimetres or more away from the cutting edge is called the *hamon*. Its form and variations in texture indicate the period, school and even the individual swordsmith who made the blade. The steel crystals in the hamon are described as either *nie* or *nioi*. Nie, or 'boiling', applies to clusters of crystals which are each distinctly visible to the naked eye, much like a coarse frost on the ground. Nioi means 'fragrance' and applies to fine crystals which cannot be individually distinguished with the eye, like smoke or the stars in the Milky Way. The late Dr Satō Kanzan has pointed out the use of the word in a visual sense in a seventeenth-century poem by Motoori Norinaga, in which the aspect of distant blossoms on mountain cherry trees against the morning sun is described as nioi.

A nie hamon can be further classified as *aranie* ('coarse' nie) or *konie* ('fine' nie). Distinct dense lines of nie within the hamon are called *kinsuji* ('golden lines'), or *inazuma* ('lightning'). Broader longitudinal banks of drifting lines are called *sunagashi*, or 'flowing sand'. Lines stretching downward towards the edge of the blade are called *ashi*, or 'legs', and small splashes of conglomerated crystals between hamon and edge are called *yō*, or 'leaves'.

The hamon on the pre-Heian period chokutō are usually defined as *suguha*, meaning straight, or *midareba*, meaning 'irregular'. However, later formations became more complex and decorative, leading to a wider vocabulary. The hamon usually starts from the point where the blade meets the tang but sometimes from a position a few centimetres along the blade. The line continues to the *kissaki*, or point section, where it turns up to meet the back of the blade. This portion of the hamon is known as the *boshi*, or 'cap'. A simple round boshi is called *maru*, whereas an irregular line is called *midare*.

The typical grain, or *jigane*, on the flat of the blade due to the thousands of layers of folded steel, can also indicate the school of swordmaking. Folded in one direction repeatedly, the grain will be longitudinal, or *masame*. In the earliest swords this is very evident, and on later Kamakura period swords of the Hōshō school of the Yamato tradition it can be almost perfectly straight, forming parallel lines along the blade. Generally, though, the steel was folded alternately in different directions, so that the grain is complex. Traditionally the grain in swords has been likened to that in wood, so that the equivalent of long grain is called *itame* and a cross-grain, with clearly defined concentrics, *mokume*. There are a multitude of variants of these definitions, just as there are many different trees and ways of cutting them to make timber.

A wavy, almost sinusoidal form of grain which later became known as *ayasugi hada* ('cryptomeria twill') is the mark of the Heian period Namihira school of Satsuma Province and the later Gassan school of Okushū Province. The finest of mokume grain has been called *nashiji hada*, meaning 'pear skin'. This most tiny interwoven complexity of steel is found on work as early as that of the middle Heian period master Munechika, whose masterpiece, Mikazuki Munechika, or 'The Quarter Moon Munechika', is today considered one of the most important swords in the world.

Itame grain can be further classified into *ōitame* ('large' itame), and *koitame* ('small' itame). There can also be mixtures of different grains: for example, a sword blade might be described as ōitame with a content of koitame and some mokume. Simple geometric lines alone cannot describe the grain in a sword blade; the effect of several crystalline steel structures should also be taken into account. A whitish shadow, either disjointed or with a distinct harmonious form, along the body of the blade is called *utsuri*, or 'reflection', since it 'reflects' the pattern of the hardened edge. This feature is found on many swords of the Heian and Kamakura periods, although it has become almost synonymous with the swords of Bizen Province made during the Kamakura period, on which it can be the most vivid and controlled. An indistinct utsuri is sometimes called *shirake*, or 'whiteness'. This hue is found on blades throughout the *kotō*, 'old swords', or ancient period (up until *c.* 1600), and especially on those of the school of the village of Seki in Mino Province during the Muromachi period.

Nie found across the ground, or *ji*, of the blade is called *jinie*. It can be spread lightly across the whole of the ji, or concentrated in patches forming dark splashes of *jifu* ('ground spots') or *sumi hada* ('charcoal skin'), or the larger patches of *namazu hada* ('catfish skin'), *Chikei* ('ground shadow') are hundreds of nie crystals forming lines associated with the grain of the steel and characterise work of the Sōshū school of the fourteenth century. Other names have been given to formations found on the work of certain schools and individual smiths, and will be discussed within their respective periods.

Sword appraisal and valuation

The late fourteenth-century history *Masu Kagami* tells that the Emperor Go Toba could judge a sword better than 'a man of the Way', so we know that there was a recognised profession of sword appraisers as long ago as the early Kamakura period. The Buddhist title, Nyūdō, of an appraiser in the Kamakura period called Nagoshi Omi Nyūdō tells us that he was embarked on a spiritual path.

Earlier works hint at the study of swords and their intrinsic beauty. For example, the *Engi Shiki* (record of the Engi era, 901–22) mentions the number of stages in sword polishing, indicating that the surface finish was considered to be important. However, the first known book on the study of blades, the *Kanchiin bon*, dates from 1316. The earliest extant copy of it was made in the thirtieth year of the Ōei era, 1423, and is kept in the national diet library of Japan. Having once been kept in the Kanchiin building of Tōji Temple, the book delineates smiths and their schools by name, period and province, and thus represents the earliest systematic study of any form of Japanese arts and crafts.

The best-known name among sword specialists in recent centuries is that of the Honami. The Honami family were appointed by the Shoguns to be official sword appraisers, or *mekiki*, in Edo, following recognition of the illustrious Honami Kōetsu (1558–1637), whose name is also known in connection with ceramics, lacquerware and the Tea Ceremony. The family were in the profession before that time, having worked as *bugyō* (an administrative grade) of swords for the Ashikagas. A copy, with many addenda, of a book first published in 1381 called the *Kiami Meizukushi* (a record of the Kiami family) and the existence of a similar meizukushi for the Nōami family dating from the time of Ashikaga Yoshimasa suggests that other arts and crafts were controlled by families, using the characters for *ami* in their name, who were sponsored by the Ashikaga Shoguns. Before the Genroku era Honami Kōtoku, Kōon, Mitsutada and others provided reliable *kanteishō* (certificates of authenticity) for swords. They would appraise swords which were unsigned, or which had lost their signatures due to shortening, and frequently inscribe the name of the smith together with their own signature or *oshigata* in gold inlay on the tangs. However, some later generations of the Honami were more flexible, and were not adverse to ascribing the work of a pupil to that of a master smith.

Honami Saburōbei Kōtoku (1554–1619) started the custom of inlaying appraisal inscriptions in gold on sword tangs. This had the effect of increasing the current market value of the swords, a situation furthered by his son, Kōson, who started the practice of evaluating swords in writing on the origami appraisal documents. Honami origami documents bear the red seal for the first character, *hon*, of the family name. The bronze seal was given to Kōtoku by Toyotomi Hideyoshi in recognition of the family's position as Tenka no Tōken Mekikijo, or 'Office for sword appraisal'. In 1611 the Honamis published the *Kotō Meizukushi*, an appraisal of swords according to province and school, and in 1719 at the behest of the eighth Shogun, Yoshimune (1684–1751), the thirteenth-generation Honami, Mitsutada, compiled the *Kyōhō Meibutsu Chō* listing what he considered to be the greatest swords in Japan (see p. 115).

Appraisers like the Honami were concerned primarily with the artistic merit in swords, but there were also sword testers who graded swords according to their cutting efficiency. In the early Edo period Yamano Kanjūrō (1594–1667), who later adopted the name Kauemon, specialised in testing swords and issuing certificates stating test results. He would also inscribe test details on the tangs of swords, sometimes inlaying the inscriptions with gold. Most extant blades bearing cutting test inscriptions are *shintō* ('new swords'), especially swords by the Edo contempories of Yamano, Izumi no Kami Kaneshige, Yamato no Kami Yasusada, Kazusa no Suke Kaneshige and Nagasone Kotetsu. The tests were conducted on condemned criminals or on their dead bodies. The testers specified ten or so cuts across various parts of the body between the hips and the shoulders, and the diagonal *kesa giri* cut down through one shoulder and across the body. Sometimes more than one body was used. A sword made by Yamato no Kami Yasusada is said to have been used to cut five bodies at one cut by Yamano Kauemon when he was sixty-four, and a broad blade by the sixteenth-century smith Kanefusa of Seki apparently cut through seven bodies. Swords were also tested by cutting bundles of straw wrapped around bamboo, and by cutting plates of iron or copper.

In 1815 Yamada Asaemon Yoshimutsu divided swords into classes by their cutting efficiency and published a list of *waza mono* ('useful swords'), *yoi waza mono* ('good useful swords'), *ō waza mono* ('great useful swords') and *saijō ō waza mono* ('greatest useful swords'). His categories are still remembered today, even though the sword is now thought of as an object of beauty rather than as a weapon of war.

1

The Yayoi and Kofun periods
c. 300 BC–*c.* AD 300   *c.* AD 300–*c.* 600

Although there are some sparse remains of iron implements found in excavations of pre-Yayoi sites, the first iron swords, together with ritual bronze weapons, were introduced into Japan from China during the Yayoi period. This was the time of the first advances in agriculture, for the original Jōmon people who had inhabited Japan for several centuries were hunters and gatherers. There was considerable intercourse between Japan and China during this period, and possibly widespread immigration. Chinese culture, with its superior technology of bronze and iron, must also have brought with it the concept of the State. Records indicate contact with China by more than thirty of the autonomous kingdoms which existed in Japan during the first century AD; and these kingdoms surely required arms. Undoubtedly, the King of Nu in Southern Japan, for example, must have been a powerful military figure for in AD 57 his emmissary to the Han court at Loyang was given a seal confirming the king's position in the name of the Chinese Emperor. The Chinese *Wei Chi* ('Chronicle of the Wei dynasty') records the arrival of an envoy from Yamatai, one of the countries of Wa (Japan) in June AD 239. The envoy was from Queen Himiko, who, in return for a tribute to the Chinese Emperor of textiles and slaves, received a gold seal naming her as an ally of Wei, gold, silks, 150 mirrors and, significantly, swords.

The few extant excavated swords, daggers and fragments of them from this period are so corroded that their exact metallurgy is unknown, but the blades were straight and flat-sided or of shallow triangular (*hira zukuri*) section, and the ends of the tangs were drawn out into bars turned to form annular pommels. These are known as *kantō tachi*, or 'ring-headed swords'.

The fashion for kantō tachi continued through the Kofun, or 'great tombs' period. At this time the warlike clans of Japan vied against each other for power, growing under the strong influence of China and Korea. The tribes moved from Kyūshū, the southern island, where the continental influence was strongest, northwards. They were unified by the Yamato, ancestors of the Imperial line, who settled near present-day Nara. The burial mounds of their leaders contain rich grave-goods, including horse-trappings and iron armour, indicating their warlike nature, similar to those found in Korean graves of the same period.

Invariably, the graves contain examples of the three objects which have remained since in the Imperial regalia – the jewel, the mirror and the sword. The swords include kantō tachi, whose blades are extended to form a ring at the end of the tang, and in later graves far more elaborate pieces decorated with silver and gold, and with separate gilt-bronze ring pommels. It is probable that at least some of the blades were forged in Japan, but many were evidently made on the mainland, as inscriptions prove. Indeed, there is evidence that even in those days Chinese blades were highly regarded. The Empress Suiko (reigned 592–628) is recorded as having said: 'For a horse chose a steed from Hyūga [a province in Kyūshū] and for a sword chose a *masabi* from Gō [a Chinese province]'.

A kantō tachi excavated from the late fourth-century tumulus at Tōdaijiyama bears an inscription which proves its origin in China. Since the sword predates the burial by two centuries, it indicates the veneration in which ancient swords were held even in those days. The twenty-four-character inscription runs from just below the point of the sword, continuing for 75.5 cm along its length. It contains an apparent astronomical reference, mention of forging and hardening, and a Chinese era, Zhongping (AD 184–9), together with a cyclical date in the month of May which could indicate either the first or fifth year of the era.

The blade of this sword, the oldest-dated sword yet found in Japan, is iron, single-edged and of hira zukuri form. It appears to have a slight downward curve in the style called *uchi zori*, or 'inner curve', which is found also on later straight swords, but this curvature might have come about as a result of the stresses caused by corrosion. The kantō itself is made of bronze, and dates from the time of the tomb. It was fixed to the end of the tang of the blade by rivets through two holes. However, the blade probably originally had a ring of iron, either integral with the tang or made separately and with the tang wrapped over it. The tomb also contained further swords, spear blades and elliptical bronze pieces which might have been parts of lacquered leather shields.

Sword-fittings
Since the Kofun period, when swords were mounted in Chinese and Korean styles using gilt-bronze, the scabbard, hilt and metal fittings have been provided by specialist

artisans. The best material for scabbards was magnolia wood, which does not exude saps or resins that might damage the blades. Different substances were probably used to coat the scabbards, like leather, rattan and textile, although nothing but traces of such organic material survive. However, the wood could be coated with lacquer, which is waterproof and strong against impact and corrosion.

Scabbards and hilts were further dressed with metal rings, chapes and pommels. These were sometimes of iron, in which case there might be some form of decoration with inlaid silver wire. The wood was further wrapped in gilt or silvered copper decorated with line engraving, or repoussé work, and sometimes bound with wire. An interesting form of *tsuba* ('sword guard') is often found. It is a flattened egg-shaped section, pierced so as to resemble an eccentric spoked wheel. This wheel shape recurs on tsuba throughout later periods.

The pommels can be the most striking part of these excavated mountings, particularly the kantō-type ring pommels. Some contain figures of birds or dragons, cast in bronze on the early Chinese pieces but often cut from plate in later Japanese examples. This latter technique of openwork in silhouette remained in use on metal sword-fittings until the end of the nineteenth century. Other types of hilt were developed in Japan – the *kabutsuchi*, or 'hammerhead' type, with a large bulbous, hollow, offset pommel, and the *keitō*, or 'jewel-head' type. These were usually gilt, and the tangs occasionally bound with wires of silver, copper or gold.

The tangs of the blades contained one or more holes so that the hilt could be attached by means of pegs or cords, and some tangs are stepped for the same purpose. A further hole in the blade just above the guard might have been used to retain the sword firmly in its scabbard when not in use, although no mechanisms for this are known to have survived.

Armour

There was undoubtedly armour in the Yayoi period, evidenced by the excavation of vermilion- and black-lacquered wooden portions of a cuirass, now in the collection of the Hamamatsu City Museum. These fragments are similar to the iron armours excavated from the tumuli of the Kofun period. There are two main types – the *tanko* and the *keiko*. Several tanko, which are formed of solid plate, survive in their original shape in relatively good condition; but the keiko consists of small plates linked together to be flexible and have not kept their original form, usually having collapsed in piles. Reconstructions have, however, been possible with reference to *haniwa*, earthenware figures, sometimes made in the form of armed warriors, which have been found embedded in the ground at the approaches to the tumuli. It is known from the dates of excavation sites that the keiko was a later development, more tanko than keiko being found in Kyūshū, and the keiko being the dominant type in the Yamato area; and it is the keiko which forms the basis for all later armour.

The tanko were cuirasses made from a number of broad iron plates linked together, at first with leather binding for flexibility, and later, in the fifth century, by rivets, to form a well-defined torso. The most prevalent type consists of large triangular plates riveted together with horizontal supporting bands, but there were also pieces formed of broad horizontal bands with vertical bracing plates. The back swelled out to cover the chest, high over the shoulders while the front was lower. Straps over the shoulders supported the armour. The tanko opened by a long hinge at the sides to close down the centre of the front. A further *akabe* consisting of two symmetric halves laced together around the neck covered the immediate top of the back and breast.

The keiko was very different from the tanko. It was composed of a large number of small vertically arrayed strips, or *kozane*, linked together in horizontal sets which were further tied in rows one above the other. These kozane could be either rectangular, elliptical or with a shallow trefoil profile. The whole hung flexibly down from the shoulders, and had a loosely hanging apron, or *kusazuri*, of the same construction. The flexible keiko is very much a horseman's armour and is found in graves together with horse-trappings. The origin of the keiko on the mainland is indicated interestingly by the use of almost identical armours as far away from Japan as Tibet in recent centuries. The keiko provided the basic form of later armour from the Heian period onwards.

Helmets of the Heian and later periods also reveal their

origins in the Kofun period. There were two main types: the first was the *shokaku tsuki kabuto* ('battering ram helmet'), which came to a protruding sharp vertical ridge at the front, like a battering ram. These helmets were first made of broad horizontal bands laced and then riveted together like the tanko, and were later formed of a larger number of narrower vertically aligned plates also riveted together. The other main type of helmet excavated from the kofun was the *mabishi tsuki kabuto* ('peaked helmet'). This type of helmet postdates the shokaku tsuki type. It

is similarly formed of riveted plates but is perfectly round in cross-section, with a decoratively shaped or pierced peak. These helmets sometimes have further decorative pieces rising from the crown, and some are made with gilt-bronze covering the iron. The neck of both types was protected by a *shikoro* of curved bands of iron, which extend from side to side around the back of the head and neck and are laced flexibly together. This feature, with slight variations in shape and size, remains a characteristic of all later Japanese helmets.

1 Sword pommel

Gilt-bronze
Late Kofun period, 6th century
H. 7.1 cm
British Museum, JA 1936, 11–18, 136

Gilt-bronze pommels of the kantō tachi mounting frequently contained dragons or phoenixes, either singly or in pairs. The phoenix of this piece is in a surround forming stylised flames. The style of roundly casting these objects originated on the continent, whereas later pieces worked in flat plate (no. 2) were a Japanese innovation.

1   *enlarged by 30%*

2

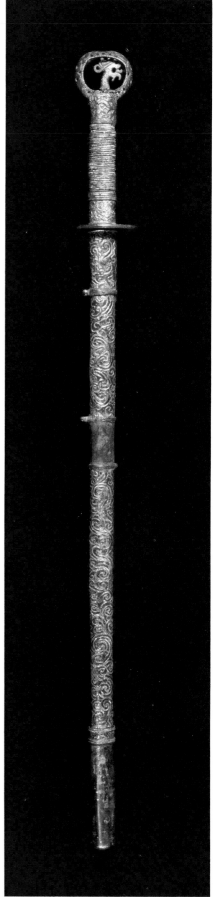

2 Pommel

Gilt-bronze
Late Kofun period, 6th–7th century
w. 8.5 cm

An excavated kashira from a chokutō
mounting, with two stylised opposed
dragons with a single jewel at their mouths.

3 Kantō tachi *(illus. in colour on p. 81)*

Kofun period, 6th–7th century
L. 92.0 cm

Both the hilt and scabbard of this rich
mounting are wrapped with thin gilt-copper
sheet. The kashira is of annular form
containing the roundly carved head and
shoulders of a dragon. It ends in a sleeve
which fits over the hilt. Both this sleeve and
the fuchi are decorated with the body of the
dragon in repoussé work. The space
between is bound with copper and gold wire
twisted together. The tsuba is of the 'egg-
shaped' type, with a high rim. On the upper
part is a design of two rows of circles,
hammered in relief, making a slight spiral.
The under-side is decorated with clouds.
The chape of the scabbard is a round-ended
plain piece. There are two bands with holes
for suspending the sword from the belt, and
on the upper of these remains a buckle. The
blade is so rusted that it cannot be drawn
from the scabbard.

The kantō tachi is the most common type
of Kofun period sword.

3   *reverse*

THE YAYOI AND KOFUN PERIODS 19

4

4 Helmet

Kofun period, 5th century; excavated from the
    Egenoyama no. 2 Tumulus, Tokushima City,
    Tokushima
H. 14.0 cm
Tokyo National Museum

The helmet is made from horizontal bands
of iron supporting five triangular plates
both left and right of the bowl, and with the
beaked ridge running from the top to the
centre of the forehead which gives it its
name, *shokaku tsuki kabuto* ('battering ram
helmet'). A decorative peak with eight
foliate sections extends horizontally from
beneath the rim at the front. Three bands of
iron, once loosely hung around the back
and sides of the helmet to protect the neck,
show clearly the origin of the later shikoro.

This type of helmet was worn with an
iron body armour of the tanko type, also
made of iron plates riveted together in a
similar structure. It was excavated from the
burial chamber of an aged man together
with other armour and weapons. The
quality of such armour symbolises the power
of the Yamato people during the Kofun and
Nara periods, and its profusion in graves of
the nobility of the time is an indication of
the prestige in which the growing military
cast was to be held in future centuries.

2

The Nara period
(AD 646–794)

The middle of the sixth century saw the introduction of Buddhism into Japan, which was to become accepted as the national religion by the seventh century, alongside the native Shintō. Buddhist temples were built in the new capital, Nara, and throughout Japan. The Taika reform of AD 645–9 promoted further close ties with China, and all kinds of Chinese technologies were absorbed.

In an effort to gain control of the northern provinces the government waged long and bitter campaigns against the Ainu, who opposed the heavily armed Yamato people with the bows and probably poisoned arrows of a hunting people. In 762 the military system was strengthened by the establishment of the *kondei* ('stalwart youth') class, which provided trained officers from among the sons of the great families. These hereditary warriors must have formed the basis of the samurai class.

In AD 782 the Emperor Kammu moved the capital away from Nara and the powerful influences of the priesthood, and established it at Heian which was later to become Kyoto. He invested heavily in the army, in 794 building the Butokukan ('Hall of Military Virtue'), which remains today in Kyoto the mecca for archers and swordsmen. The final defeat of organised Ainu opposition occurred in AD 792 by an army led by Saka no Ue Tamura Maro (AD 758–811), whose sword, a chokutō, is preserved today in Kurama Temple.

Other Chinese and Japanese chokutō have survived from this period, in the collections of temples and shrines. Like the mirror the sword is significant in Buddhism, both being the attributes of deities. In Shintō, however, either might be revered as the *shintai* itself, the actual physical manifestation of the kami, or resident deity of the shrine, like the sword known as Futsu No Mitama Ōken, the deity of Kashima Shrine.

Two examples of such preserved chokutō which have been polished in recent years are the so-called Heishi Shōrin Ken and Shichi Sei Ken ('Seven Stars Sword') from the Shitennōji Temple collection. They are both of well-forged steel with almost straight hamon, of *katakiri ha* construction, with a *shinogi* (ridge) line on one side of the blade nearer the cutting edge than the back, and with slight uchi zori curvature. Shitennōji Temple tradition has it that the swords belonged to Shōtoku Taishi (AD 574–622), the devout Buddhist prince who instituted

nationwide reforms in education, foreign affairs, religion, law and government during the period of his regency.

Fifty-five chokutō are in the collection of the Shōsōin in Nara. This repository for the Tōdaiji Temple was built by the Empress Kōmyō to house the personal effects of the Emperor Shōmu, who died in AD 756. Also in the collection are thirty-eight *hoko*, a kind of glaive, and seventy small knives called *tōsu*. Tōsu are single-edged blades only a few centimetres in length, forged like the chokutō and with hamon. Some are mounted singly, others in sets with wood scabbards. The Taihō code of AD 701, which adopted Chinese systems of administration and legislation, and other records suggest that tōsu were a symbol of rank and were carried by both men and women.

The kissaki of the Kofun period swords was single-edged, but in the Nara period a new type having a return edge stretching partly along the back of the blade, known as *kissaki moroha*, was introduced. Most have a downward curve, or uchi zori, with the cutting edge slightly concave. A fine example of this type originally in the Shōsōin collection, known as the Suiryū Ken, or 'Water Dragon Sword' (see no. 5), after the Imperial Restoration of 1876 passed into the hands of the Emperor Meiji who commissioned Kanō Natsuo (see pp. 116–17, nos 133, 134) to make a rich mounting for it, decorated with dragons among waves in gold and silver.

Generally the chokutō had a single hole, or *mekugi ana*, through the tang to accommodate a cord, or later a wooden peg, which secured the wooden hilt. The first swords with a curvature away from the cutting edge were made in the Nara period. A number of swords in the Shōsōin are of a type called *musōtō*, or 'mountless', with no hole in the tang for securing a hilt. These swords occur in lengths varying between 30 cm and 1 m. Many of their tangs are broad and swell out at each end, so that they could be bound perhaps with rattan to provide a grip. A fine example in the collection is 106 cm long. The base of the blade broadens slightly over the bottom few centimetres, and the top portion has a slight curvature away from the edge. The jigane of this sword is fine itame with masame along the edge. The hamon is suguha in nie, with ashi and *hotsure* ('fraying'), and forms *nijuba* (a double hamon line) in the upper part of the blade. These features evolved into the more readily recognisable characteristics of the later Yamato school, which became prominent in the thirteenth century.

There is one example of another kind of sword called a *warabite tachi*, or 'young fern hilt sword', in the Shōsōin collection, although many have been excavated. Warabite tachi have deeply angled tangs turned over at the tip in a shape reminiscent of the delicacy *warabi*, fern shoots plucked before the leaf has unfolded. The tangs were further bound with rattan or similar material. Some of these swords have guards formed as part of the blade. They are shorter and broader than most chokutō and, in addition to the curve in the hilt afforded by the deep angle of the tang, they are often slightly curved, a number being of kissaki moroha type. Some warabite tachi have their tangs pierced by a longitudinal slot. This might have been simply for fixing the hilt but could have provided a cushioning effect for shock transmitted along the blade when armour was struck, for these were evidently intended primarily as cutting weapons.

Sword-fittings

Together with technical improvements in the method of manufacture, and the appearance of different types of blade during the Nara period, there were two great changes in the mountings of tachi. First, the custom of wrapping scabbards in metal gave way to the use of lacquer, and secondly the huge pommels dissappeared. Although few mountings survive from the Nara period, those that do clearly fall into two main types – the simple mounting for the active military, and sumptuously mounted blades for the aristocracy.

The chokutō mounting in the Kurama Temple collection which belonged to General Sakaue Tamura Maro is sombrely lacquered black. Its metal fittings are small and light, clearly the predecessors of the mountings of the later curved tachi. Several different kinds of mountings are mentioned in the *Tōdaiji Kenmotsu Chō* to describe the weapons kept in the Shōsōin repository. There were *inhōken* (yin 'treasure sword'), *yōhōken* (yang 'treasure sword'), *kondōsō kara tachi* ('gilt-bronze decorated Chinese sword') and *kingin densō kara tachi* ('gold and silver decorated Chinese sword'). Although many of the Shōsōin swords were removed in AD 764 to be used in the

campaign of the subjugation of the Emi, and in most cases different replacements returned, the kingin densō kara tachi is clearly identifiable. It is a chokutō once carried by the Emperor Shōmu, richly mounted with a decorative lacquer scabbard, and gold and silver metalwork pierced with scrolling and inset with jewels. The hilt is covered with the hardened white skin of the ray fish, which became used on all kinds of mountings from the Heian period.

The richer scabbards of the Nara period swords were decorated with *makie*, or gold dust shaken on to the lacquer, and often shell inlay. One short tachi in the Shōsōin is decorated on the scabbard with *heidatsu*, metal inlay level with the surface of the lacquer. The scabbards are flat in section, reflecting the newly developed katakiri ha-type blade construction.

Horimono ('carved decoration')

The earliest forms of decoration found on the swords of the Kofun and Nara periods are inscriptions like that on the Tōdaijiyama sword (p. 15), and the Heishi Shōrin Ken (p. 20). The latter has four Chinese characters engraved and inlaid with gold on the base of the blade. Heishi represents a cyclical date, and Shōrin is thought to be a name. The inscription is inlaid into a cut groove, or *hi*, the purpose of which is primarily to lighten the blade and yet retain its rigidity. The Shichi Sei Ken is engraved with the seven stars motif of Chinese astronomical religion, found also on one of the Shōsōin swords, together with the shape of a dragon's head.

Armour

Both the tanko and keiko of the Kofun period are mentioned in the Nara period *Nihon Shōki* ('The Chronicles of Japan', AD 720), which names the separate components of the armour including the shoulder-pieces (*kata yoroi*), sleeves (*kote, taori* or *temari*), knee protectors (*hiza yoroi*) and calf protectors (*suneate*). Pieces recorded in the *Tōdaiji Kenmotsu Chō* (an inventory of the Tōdaiji Temple treasures kept in the Shōsōin, AD 756) no longer exist in the collection, and it is likely that they were not returned after being used in the campaigns against the Ainu. A simpler form of armour for low-ranking soldiers was the Chinese-style *menoko*, which consisted of iron plates fitted on to a cotton coat.

5 Suiryū Ken ('Water Dragon Sword')

Nara period, 8th century; early Yamato school
L. 62.1 cm
Tokyo National Museum, Important Cultural
Property

This sword was originally in the collection
of the Shōsōin, Nara, and is thought to have
been worn by the Emperor Shōmu whose
effects were enshrined in the building by
his widow, the Empress Kōmyō, in AD 756.
During the Meiji period the sword was
mounted in *hōken*, or 'treasure sword', style
by Kanō Natsuō (1828–98), to the personal
requirement of the Emperor Meiji. It is a
finely forged katakiri ha chokutō blade of
bright steel, with uchi zori curve, flowing
itame hada showing white shadows in
places, and a gently varying suguha. Among
the Shōsōin swords of dignified pedigree, it
is a particularly robust and beautiful blade,
and must have delighted the sword-loving
Emperor. Made in Nara in the eighth century
in an intense Buddhist environment, it can
be considered as one of the earliest blades
in the Yamato tradition. An interesting
comparison can be made with the Heian
period tachi called Shishi-Ō (no. 7), which
also has suguha and similar white shadows
on the blade, and which exemplifies the
Yamato tradition in transitional curved
blades.

3

The Heian period

(AD 794–1185)

The Heian period describes the four centuries during which Japan was governed by the aristocracy in Kyoto. This was the time of the flowering of a purely Japanese culture, when Japan relaxed her ties with China. However, during most of the eleventh and twelfth centuries the great clans vied with each other and against powerful Buddhist sects for Imperial favour, which brought influence in government and lands in the provinces. Armies were kept by the provincial lords, the great clans, and monasteries like Tōdaiji, Hiezan and Koya. A series of civil wars culminated in 1184 with a victory of the Minamoto clan over the Taira and the establishment of the military government at Kamakura in 1185.

The deeply curved sword of the samurai developed some time during the middle to late Heian period. It is undoubtedly a more efficient cutting weapon than a straight sword, especially when wielded single-handed by a horseman. Heian period curved swords are of much harder steel than the old straight blades, resulting from more advanced methods of forging and heat treating. The shinogi is nearer the back of the blade, so that the triangular section is a shallow angle, forming a sharper edge. Stresses arising from hammering the blade into this sharper section would tend to form a curve, and a further curve is induced during the quenching process in the hardening heat treatment itself. So it is at least in part true to say that the curve arises naturally as the result of more sophisticated manufacturing methods, although the final shape was carefully regulated.

Although it is not clear exactly when the first curved swords were made, a number of blades which might be regarded as transitional remain from the early Heian period. A tachi in the Imperial Household collection called Kogarasu Maru, or 'Little Crow', seems to owe something of its shape to the warabite tachi (see p. 21). It is a broad kissaki moroha-type blade with a return edge extending about halfway along the back, and is carved with grooves either side, extending along the length of the blade. It is deeply curved at the tang and has a slight, even curve along its length. The blade is thought to have been given to the Emperor Kammu (781–806) by a priestess of the Ise Shrine, and later passed into the hands of Taira Sadamori as a reward for his victory over Fujiwara Sadatomo in the Heiji wars between the great Fujiwara

and Taira clans. However, this sword is of a unique shape, and its place in the transitional process is far from evident.

More obviously transitional is the *kenuki gata tachi*, the tang of which forms the hilt, integral with the blade, and is pierced with a longitudinal slot like that found on some warabite tachi. This type of sword is either straight or of shallow curve in the upper part of the blade but broadens somewhat at the lower part and curves markedly along the hilt. It has a clear shinogi either side, and usually along the middle of the flat of the blade or higher. An example preserved in the Ise Shrine belonged to Tawara Toda, who was appointed governor of Shimotsuke Province in the Engi era (AD 901–22), so the style dates back at least until the beginning of the tenth century. The sword could, of course, be older, since old swords were prized even in those days. A similar example shown in the Kamakura period portrait of the Shogun Fujiwara Yoritomo in the collection of the Jingoji Temple was possibly 200 years old in Yoritomo's time. (There is a contemporary version of this portrait in the British Museum, JA 1920.7–13.1.)

It is likely that the swords of the Nara period were made in or around Nara, probably in association with temples, and can be considered the beginnings of the Yamato tradition. The jigane of the chokutō often has a flowing, or masame appearance, with a white sheen along the blade. The hamon is usually straight, yet with unevenness and variation. These characteristics remain on some kenuki gata tachi. A typical sword in this style, which indicates the origins of the later Yamato tradition, is the curved tachi known as Shishi-Ō ('Lion King'), which tradition has it was given to Minamoto Yorimasa in gratitude for his killing the Nue, a monster which had brought a sickness upon the Emperor Nijō (no. 7). This sword has a powerful, yet elegant shape: it has a high shinogi, the blade decreases in width from base to point, the kissaki is small, and the curve is deep at the base of the blade, while the upper portion remains almost straight. The shape has changed somewhat due to polishing, but if the line of the shinogi on the tang is followed along the blade, it will be seen that it must have originally been closer to the cutting edge. However, few such swords survive, and the Yamato school seems to have lost prominence before the rising schools of Kyoto, Kibi, Kyūshū and other provinces, until the tentative identification of Yamato smiths like Senshuin Yukinobu and Shigehirō at the beginning of the twelfth century.

By the twelfth century schools had been established in several provinces, and many elegant fully curved swords survive from this period with distinctive forging grain and hamon. These include signed works by eminent smiths such as Yasutsuna of Hōki (no. 10), Sanjō Munechika of Kyoto, Masatsune and Tomonari of Bizen (no. 9) and Miike Mitsuyo of Chikugo.

Some of the major centres of swordmaking were near the supplies of iron ore. In an important position were the lands lying along the coastal roads, Sanindō and Sanyōdō, which ran north and south of the Chūgoku region of Honshū, the main island, and which were major routes between Kyūshū and central Japan. The area richest in iron deposits was Kibi on the Sanyōdō. Kibi had been a major iron producer during the Kofun period. The classical anthology of poems, the *Kokon Waka Shū* (*c.* AD 905) tells of 'Nakayama in Kibi, where the iron comes from'; and the *Engi Shiki* (*c.* AD 927) tells us that 'paddy fields are tilled with iron hoes from Kibi'. At the end of the seventh century Kibi was divided into three provinces – Bitchū, Bingo and Bizen – and a further inland area, Mimasaka, was defined in AD 713.

Masatsune and Tomonari of Bizen Province (present-day Okayama Prefecture) had access to a magnetic ore called *satetsu* (literally sand iron) brought from Mimasaka. Known as *akame*, or 'red stuff', it differed from the ores of Bitchū. The jigane of Tomonari's swords is fine and close packed, with clear white utsuri. The hamon is of konie and is characteristically of a form called *chōji*, or 'cloves', since it resembles a row of bunched buds of clove flowers. There seem to have been several generations signing the name Tomonari, all fine sword makers (no. 9). Blades of the Ko Aoe (Old Aoe) school of Bitchū have their distinctive hada known as *chirimen* resembling a kind of silk crepe of that name, with bright konie spread evenly over the surface.

Yasutsuna of Hōki Province was the maker of the sword known as Dōjigiri, a National Treasure regarded during the Edo period as the greatest of Japanese swords. It was used by Minamoto Yorimitsu to quell the Shuten Dōji, a monstrous fiend, or more probably a ferocious highwayman. The Dōjigiri sword was numbered among

the Tenka Gōken ('Five Best Swords Under Heaven') since the Muromachi period. These included Onimaru ('The Demon') by Kunitsuna of the Awataguchi school in Heian (Kyoto), Mikazuki ('The Quarter Moon') by Munechika, Juzumaru ('The Rosary') by Tsunetsugu of the Ko Aoe school, and Ō Tenta ('Great Tenta') by Tenta Mitsuyo. These swords are all of the late Heian period and are work of the leading smiths of the earliest established schools.

The jigane, or hada, of Yasutsuna's swords stands out more than the fine-grained work of the Bizen smiths. It contains dark pools of steel, with lines of chikei and jifu utsuri. The hamon is almost wholly a wild midareba, abundant in activity with kinsuji and sunagashi. Yasutsuna's work seems perhaps earlier, and certainly less sophisticated than that of Tomonari of Bizen, yet it possesses a wild beauty that seems beyond mere human contrivance.

Sanjō Munechika of Kyoto, regarded as the founder of the Yamashiro school, made elegantly shaped swords with fine jigane, and midareba-type hamon rich in activity, yet delicate and refined. A feature of his work is the *uchi no ke* formation of upward-pointing lines of crescent-moon shape on the edge of the hamon. It is probably from these that his masterpiece, Mikazuki (see p. 13), derives its name, rather than the shape of the blade.

The swords of the Heian period are long and slender. The kissaki are small, and the blades gradually widen towards the hilt, then curve deeply and widen abruptly at the base, or *koshi* (the 'waist' of the blade). This type of curve is called *koshi zori*, and although it is found on all late Heian period tachi, it became particularly identified with the swords of Bizen and has been called Bizen zori. The broadening of the blade at the koshi is known as *fumbari*, meaning 'tenacity', or 'bottom'. The blades feel light in the hand, although some are of massive proportions. A typical length is from 75 to 80 cm, although some are longer. The tangs form a continuous curve with the blades, although some are further abruptly curved away from the edge. Shorter swords, like the *isshaku amari no uchigatana* ('cutting swords about 30 cm long') mentioned in the *Azuma Kagami* ('Mirror of the East', 1266), were also made, although few survive.

In addition, there were daggers, called *koshigatana* ('waist swords'), or *koshimono* ('waist things'), but the only signed specimens known are one signed Tomonari of Bizen in the collection of the Itsukushima Shrine and a katakiri ha blade signed Munechika belonging to the Tokugawa Reimeikai. However, these are both *saiba*, meaning that they have at some time been retempered, so that their original hamon is lost. Other weapons included the broad-bladed pole-arms called *naginata*, a kind of glaive, thought to be used in the wars between the Taira and Minamoto, but no examples are known to have survived.

The *ken*, a double-edged blade, makes its appearance during the Heian period. The ken was made in various lengths, but many short examples were made for use in exorcism and such ceremonies of esoteric Buddhism, and are mounted in hilts in the form of a three-pronged *vajra*, like the weapon held by the deity Fudō Myō-Ō (p. 27). Early ken swell out somewhat at the head, like the ritual bronze weapons imported from China in the Yayoi period; but later pieces, from the Kamakura period onward, are usually straight-sided, with or without a *yokote* line dividing the flat of the blade from the kissaki section.

Sword-fittings

The kingin densō kara tachi of the Nara period developed into the *kazari* ('decorative') tachi for formal use at court during the Heian period. The blades of these purely ceremonial swords were often little more than slender bars of iron, since they were not intended for combat. The scabbards were correspondingly narrow and either straight or of shallow curve, and richly decorated with gold makie lacquerwork and inlay of metal and mother-of-pearl. The metal pommels and chapes were long pieces of gilt-copper openwork, although more luxurious pieces could be of solid gold and studded with jewels. The style remained fixed for several hundred years, and although only a few specimens survive from the Heian period, Edo period examples (no. 12) adhere closely to the original designs.

Kenuki gata tachi remained in use during the Heian period, their integral iron hilts becoming more sumptuously sculpted. Their scabbards were either lacquered or covered with brocade. A few examples survive of tachi wrapped with helical bands of metal throughout their length: the hilt of a tachi in the Sanage Shrine is wrapped with gilt-copper in this manner. The

fashion re-emerged from time to time, and was sometimes used on scabbards during the Momoyama period.

During the late Heian period tachi lacquered black overall were popular with the military and priesthood, like Minamoto Raikō's sword named Shishi-Ō (no. 8). Hilts were bound with braid, leather strip or rattan. Scabbards were of wood, sometimes covered first with leather and then lacquered. Tsuba were either *yamagane* (literally 'mountain metal'), or unrefined copper, or formed of several layers of compressed leather. The style is found during later periods sometimes on *handachi* (literally 'half' tachi) which were carried through the belt, and sometimes on uchigatana mountings. Shorter uchigatana-type swords both with and without tsuba existed in this period, but no complete pieces survive.

The form of the tachi mounting was thus established in the Heian period, and with some variation in type it remained in use by armoured samurai right through to the Edo period. Like the scabbards the hilts were made of wood and usually wrapped with the skin of the ray fish, which is hard and long-lasting and provides an excellent grip. Metal fittings on the hilt included the *kabuto gane* (pommel) and *fuchi* (collar around the base of the hilt). On some very early swords there was a row of rivets arranged to contact the edge of the tang to hold it in place, but these became decorative *kazari byō* on later ceremonial weapons. Two decorative pieces called *menuki* were positioned either side of the tang to aid the handgrip. Below the tsuba there would be a *kuchi kanamono*, a metal collar around the mouth of the scabbard corresponding to the fuchi on the hilt. A similar band called a *semegane* strengthened the scabbard in its lower part. The tip of the scabbard was fitted with a matching chape, or *ishizuki*. Two *yaguragane* attached to further bands around the scabbard provided fixtures for the carrying cords.

Horimono

Grooves running the whole length of the blade were cut after the sword was finished for mechanical purposes, but they none the less added aesthetically to the appearance of the sword. Some smiths, like Yasutsuna and Munechika, never made horimono, but others carved both grooves and religious themes on their blades.

Yukihira of Bungo Province carved small images on the

shinogi ji at the koshi of his blades. Sometimes these were carved inside long grooves, or *bohi*, which extended the length of the blade. There has been some discussion about the identity of figures carved by Yukihira. A human standing on a rock has been called Fudō Myō-Ō, and also the Bodhisattva Jizō. Fudō Myō-Ō was significant for both swordsmith and samurai alike. The Shingon sect deity sits in flames, his face in a terrifying grimace, holding a *kensaku* rope in one hand and a sword in the other. The sword is a ken-type double-edged blade mounted with a hilt in the form of a vajra. His kensaku is to bind illusion, the enemy of Buddhism, and his sword is to cut through the illusory world to reveal the ultimate truth of the *kongōtai*, the nothingness of Zen. His name means 'Unmoving' and symbolises the spiritual attitude sought by the samurai who had to be ready to face death at any moment.

The sword of Fudō Myō-Ō might also be itself depicted as a small carving at the koshi of a blade. Yukihira and Tomonari of Bizen sometimes carved this so-called *suken* ('simple sword'), which remained popular thereafter. Another of Yukihira's favoured horimono was the *kurikara*, Fudō Myō-Ō's sword entwined by his kensaku in the form of a dragon.

Armour

When mounted, the main weapon of the samurai during this period was the long bow. It is taller than a man, but unlike its European counterpart the Japanese bow has a grip set about one-third the way up its length. This is to facilitate carrying the weapon from side to side across the horse's head, bringing it to bear on enemies to right and left. The arrows are commensurately long, with large steel heads of various shapes. Japanese horses stand short, yet are robust and game. Trained to run smoothly, they maintained constant contact with the ground, so as not to disturb the aim of the archer. The samurai rode in a wooden saddle shaped to support his thighs when he stood in stirrups formed of long platforms which support the whole foot (no. 14). He could therefore stand firmly to loose his arrows, or make cuts with his sword.

The keiko developed into the classic 'great harness', or *ōyoroi*, of the late Heian period and continued in use during the Kamakura period (no. 19). It was designed very much with protection against arrows in mind. Originally

the expression ōyoroi referred to the cuirass only, and a complete armour was called a *yoroi soroe*, consisting of a helmet, a cuirass with an apron attached, two ō sode, or shoulder pieces, a hiza yoroi, suneate and kote (see p. 21).

The cuirass is formed of horizontal rows of slender lacquered iron plates, or kozane, linked together by braid so as to be flexible and absorb impact like the keiko of the Kofun and Nara periods. It fits around the body on four sides and is secured on the right. A further rectangular piece, or *waidate*, similarly composed of rows of linked kozane, covers the join on the right side of the trunk. An iron piece across the top of the breast, the *munaita*, provides a more solid defence for the upper parts. The front of the cuirass is covered with a piece of leather, the *tsurubashiri*, or 'bow-string run', to provide a smooth surface for the bow string to travel over. The kusazuri, is composed of rows of linked lamellae similar to the cuirass, at front, back and sides. This hangs somewhat more flexibly than the cuirass, so that it can ride up in front of the saddle to protect the lower abdomen and allow the legs freedom of movement to the sides. Two flaps, the *sendan no ita* and the *kyubi no ita*, hang in front of the shoulders over the braces of the cuirass. That on the left, the kyubi no ita, is a single piece which falls into position to protect the left armpit when the bow is levelled to shoot. The two ō sode likewise provide the service of great shields to cover the extended arm and shoulders. The kote, worn on the left arm since the right had to be unimpeded in order to aim arrows, had integral gauntlets and consisted of chain-mail mounted on textile with iron plates on the lower and upper arms.

The helmet bowl is formed of a number of wrought-iron plates, usually between ten and thirty-two, riveted together vertically. The norm was a *hoshi kabuto* ('star helmet'), with the rivet ends protruding outward in rows. To the helmet bowl was attached a shikoro. Composed of linked rows of lamellae, like the apron, it was designed to provide ample cover for the neck and shoulders, and yet be flexible enough to allow freedom of movement of the head. The shikoro folded easily to allow the arms to be raised above the head in order to make a two-handed downward cut with the sword. Shikoro are also found on some excavated helmets of the Kofun period (no. 4). At the two ends of the shikoro two large flaps called *fukigaeshi* turn back forming a double layer of extra cover. The fukigaeshi, shikoro, ō sode and kyubi no ita all fell together forming a wall of protection between the helmet and the cuirass when the arm was raised to use the bow.

Suneate protected the lower legs, and hiza yoroi covered also the knees. Although there are no examples known to have survived from the Heian period, their form, which recurred in later centuries, is known from sources like the thirteenth-century *Heiji Monogatari Ekotaba* ('The Illustrated Tales of the Heiji Wars') scroll.

6 Tachi blade

Heian period, 10th–11th century
L. 70.0 cm

From its shape this sword is evidently a rare early transitional piece. The shinogi ji is wide, and the upper part of the blade is quite straight, with the straight-edged kissaki inherited from the chokutō era. The curve, almost wholly in the bottom part of the blade, owes much to the abrupt broadening, or fumbari, which remains a distinct feature of the curved sword up to the Kamakura period. The jigane is flowing itame, with stretches of masame, rich in jinie and with nie utsuri and chikei. The first nine centimetres or so of the hamon are broad and indistinct in nie, continuing into a medium suguha with small midare and sunagashi in places. From the monouchi upwards the nioi line becomes tighter and develops small ashi.

Both the shape and blade characteristics compare interestingly with the tachi named Shisho-Ō (no. 7), also a transitional sword in the early Yamato tradition.

7 Shishi-Ō ('Lion King')

Heian period, 12th century
L. 77.3 cm
Tokyo National Museum, Important Cultural
  Property

This tachi was given to Minamoto
Yorimasa, hero of the Hōgen, Heiji and
Seichi disturbances, by the Emperor Nijō.
Legend has it that Yorimasa received the
sword in reward for his having killed the
mysterious Nue, an ape-like beast with a
tail in the form of a snake, and the cause of
the Emperor's long sickness, and this theme
recurs in popular romance.

It is difficult to be certain of the date of
the blade, but in shape it has all the
appearance of a transitional curved sword.
The curve is deep at the tang and lower
part of the blade, which is almost straight in
the upper part. The shinogi is high, in
typical Yamato style; and if the line of the
shinogi along the tang is followed along
the blade, it can be seen that repolishing
over the ages has slightly changed the shape
of the sword, narrowing the shinogi ji, which
would originally have run almost along the
centre of the blade. The jihada is a flowing
itame with a straight hamon having konie,
reminiscent of the older Nara period straight
swords (no. 5). The mounting (no. 8) is
contemporary with the blade.

8 Shishi-Ō tachi mounting

Heian period, 12th century
L. 102.5 cm
Tokyo National Museum, Important Cultural
  Property

The mounting for no. 7 is lacquered black
overall, including the metal fittings, the
wood or leather tsuba, and the ray-fish skin
hilt wrapping. The silk binding is missing
from the hilt, but it would originally have
matched that over the brocade wrapping on
the upper part of the scabbard. This type of
mount is called a *hira tachi*, since the
scabbard is flatter in section than the later
elliptical fashion. The sword is an important
early example of a Heian period tachi
mounting in a style which remained in
standard use by mounted samurai from the
Heian to the Muromachi periods.

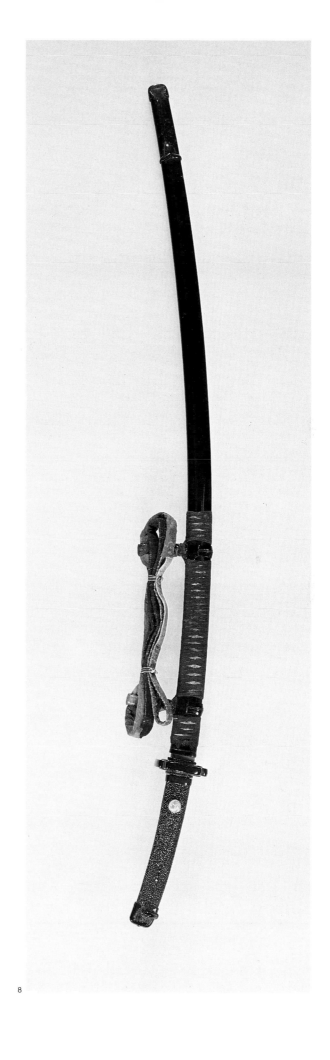

9

9 Tachi blade

Heian period, 11th century; Ko Bizen school
Signed: Bizen Kuni Tomonari
L. 79.1 cm
Tokyo National Museum

This blade is of typical Heian period form, slender, with fumbari, koshi zori and a small kissaki. The jigane is close-packed itame with jinie. The hamon is suguha with small midare, ashi, yō and kinsuji, with deep nioi and small nie. The boshi is a delicate midare komi with komaru and a little nijuba.

Tomonari is one of the first-known smiths of Bizen Province. This blade is a fine early example, although there were later generations of smiths signing Tomonari. It was given to the Emperor Meiji by the Sakai family of Himeji.

10 Tachi blade *(illus. on p. 34)*

Heian period, 11th century
Signed: Yasutsuna (Yasutsuna of Hōki Province)
L. 71.7 cm
Tokyo National Museum, Important Art Object

Although early records place Yasutsuna of Hōki at the beginning of the ninth century, active during the Daidō era (AD 806–9), there is at present insufficient material evidence to confirm that the fully curved sword was developed that early. Several examples of Yasutsuna's work survive; the Japanese National Treasure blade known as Dōjigiri Yasutsuna has been respected as being among the five best blades in Japan, though among the five it is outstanding for the strange uncontrived nature of its beauty. The name derives from the legend that Minamoto Yorimitsu killed a monster known as the Shuten Dōji, though this story seems to be unsubstantiated in early literature.

Although perhaps not such a masterpiece as the Dōjigiri, this blade bears an identical signature and has similar characteristics which mark it unmistakably as the work of the same master smith. The blade is in original form, having never been cut down. In overall shape it has a rather deeper curve than the classic Heian period type (cf. no. 9), but is otherwise typical in having a small kissaki section, the blade narrowing towards the kissaki, and having a sudden broadening and deepening just above the tang. The forging grain is large itame throughout and continuous over the shinogi ji. The hamon starts indistinctly in the base of the blade just above the *hamachi* (see p. 114), and develops into a midareba of nie rich in variation with chōji-like structures and with kinsuji and similar lines. The midare utsuri is white and sporadic, interspersed among deep dark pools of chikei. The boshi is rather indistinct, although there are lines of disjointed temper visible deep into the kissaki and parallel with its edge.

This tachi was once the property of the Matsudaira family of Echizen Province.

11 Ken blade *(illus. on p. 35)*

Heian period, 11th–12th century; Bizen school
Signed: Kanehira
L. 22.2 cm

This double-edged ken-type blade has the slight swell at the base and head characteristic of early pieces, perhaps inherited from the ritual Chinese bronze weapons of the Yayoi period, and a central groove on the shinogi either side. The jigane is itame with mokume, and flowing into masame in places, rich in jinie. The hamon is a shallow notare with small midare and gunome, deep in nioi and with nie. The boshi ends in yakitsume style at the shinogi.

There appear to have been several smiths using the name Kanehira in the Heian and Kamakura periods. Some signed with large characters, like the maker of the famous blade Ō Kanehira, and others with small characters. Ken were mostly used in religious ritual, but this example is known to have been carried as a weapon by Hirai Yasumasa, trusted retainer of Minamoto Yorimitsu.

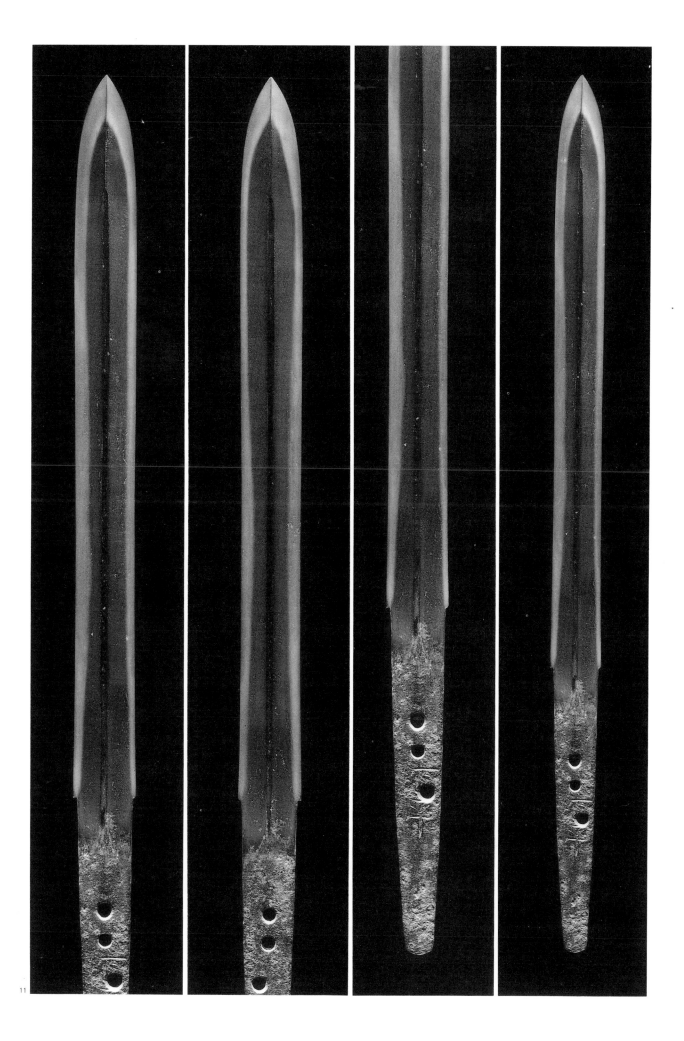

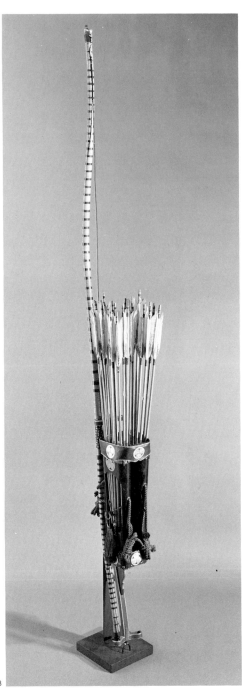

12 Kazari tachi mounting

Edo period, 19th century
L. 103.7 cm
Tokyo National Museum

This style of mounting was originally based on the kingin densō kara tachi like that in the Shōsōin collection (p. 21). It was intended for ceremonial use at court and has remained virtually unchanged since the Heian period. The scabbard of this tachi is gold-lacquered nashiji with shell inlay in the form of the circled crane design, which also occurs on parts of the gilt metalwork. The gilt floral-openwork metal pieces are studded at intervals with cloisonnés of enamel in relief, while a row of the same cloisonnés along the under-edge of the hilt reflects an ancient method of securing the blade in the hilt by a row of decorative pins, or *tawara byō* (literally 'rice bale pins', from the early typical shape). The blue-enamel drops on this example are alternatives to the lapis lazuli which was used on the higher-quality early mountings of the same type. The blades in these mountings are typically simple untempered iron pieces, being meant only for ceremonial use.

13 Bow and arrows

Edo period, 19th century
L. (bow) 220.5 cm; (arrows) 92.0 cm
British Museum, JA OA + 999

Two detachable quivers of arrows are mounted on a stand which has provision to carry two bows, one of which remains. The quivers are lacquered black, with the triple hollyhock leaf mon in gold. The compound bow is lacquered and bound with rattan, and like the arrows it is of a form virtually unchanged since the Heian period. The hand-grip of the bow is set low, owing to its great length.

14

14 Saddle and stirrups

Dated: Eiroku Juichi Nen Shogatsu Hi (a day in
    January 1568)
Signed (saddle): Sadanori and with maker's mark
H. (front piece) 27.3 cm; (rear piece) 25.8 cm; (seat)
    38.4 cm; (stirrups) 28.8 cm
Tokyo National Museum

Saddle and stirrups are decorated with
sailing ships in gold and silver high-relief
makie on a nashiji ground and with details
in gold leaf. The vertical arms of the iron
stirrups are pierced with waves, and the face
of each forms a billowing sail.

The shape of both saddle and stirrups was
established during the Heian period, to
remain unchanged save for minor variations
in style until the nineteenth century.
Although the saddle is dated in accordance
with 1568, it is likely that the lacquer
decoration was made in the early Edo period.

15

15 Ōyoroi

Nambokuchō period, 14th century
H. (cuirass) 32.0 cm; (kusazuri) 31.2 cm; (helmet
  bowl) 14.0 cm
Kagoshima Shrine Collection, Kagoshima
  Prefecture, Important Cultural Property

Although this armour dates from the
Nambokuchō period, it is in the continuing
style of ōyoroi which was established in the
late Heian period. The main innovations
made during the Kamakura period which are
evident on this piece are in the helmet.
Earlier Heian period examples invariably
have a larger hole (*tehen no ana*) in the crown
formed where the vertical plates making up
the helmet bowl meet. This was so that the
hair could be wrapped up in a cloth cap
which was pushed through the hole to hold
the helmet in place. During the Kamakura
period the number of plates making up the
helmet increased from typically ten or so to
a greater number like the twenty-eight on
this example. The projecting rivets became
correspondingly smaller. The fukigaeshi
after the Heian period usually lie flatter back
along the shikoro. The linked kozane plates
are made of lacquered leather and iron. Large
portions of the decorative leatherwork on
the armour have been accurately restored
and add to the splendour of the piece.
Inscriptions on the kuwagata indicate that
the helmet originally belonged to a different
suit, but the custom of exchanging helmets
in friendship in the field was widespread;
the armour is in remarkable condition and a
fine example of its period.

4

The Kamakura period
(1185–1333)

Ancient rivalries between the great clans which had persisted throughout the latter part of the Heian period, from time to time resulting in open warfare, came to a climax with a defeat for the Taira clan in 1185. After a series of victories the Minamoto defeated their old rivals in a sea battle at Dan-no-Ura and established themselves as the first of the military governments. Minamoto Yorimoto had himself proclaimed Shogun and set up his headquarters at the town of Kamakura, calling it the Bakufu, or 'Camp Curtain Government'. The Minamoto Bakufu ruled from Kamakura between 1185 and 1219, when Yoshitoki of the Hōjō clan wrested control from them and became Shogun himself.

Early

During the first decades of the Kamakura period the shape of the tachi was similar to that of the late Heian period. The traditions of the schools established in the Heian period in Kyūshū, Bitchū, Bizen and Yamashiro continued to prosper. Good swords were demanded not just by samurai but also by the priesthood and nobility. One of the Tenka Gōken (a Muromachi period selection of the best five blades in Japan), named Juzumaru ('The Rosary') by Tsunetsugu of Bitchū, was carried by the priest Nichiren Shōnin, the founder of the Buddhist sect named after him.

The Imperial family have also loved swords, and one emperor even worked at the craft himself. The cloistered Emperor Go Toba In (1180–1239) had attempted to overthrow the Hōjō and regain real governing power. Instead, his forces were defeated in 1221, and a new emperor, Gohorikawa, was enthroned. Go Toba In lived on for twenty years exiled to the island of Oki, during which time he devoted his energies to the study of swords. A number of swordmakers from the dominant schools were enrolled as *gō ban kaji*, smiths in rotational attendance on the Emperor. Predominantly from the schools of Bizen, Bitchū and Yamashiro, they visited Go Toba In in turn, aiding and instructing him in his art. A fourteenth-century document, the *Kanchiin Bon* (see p. 13), lists a number of smiths who attended the Emperor during a one-year period, and two specialist polishers, Kunihiro and Tamesada, each with an assistant. The smiths were Norimune, Nobufusa, Muneyoshi, Sukemune and Yukimune from Bizen, then Tsunetsugu, Sadatsugu,

Tsuguie and Sukenobu of Bitchū, and Kunisayu and Kunitomo of the Awataguchi school of Yamashiro. Other sources include also smiths from Bungo, Hōki and Mimasaka.

Norimune is considered to have been a major figure, if not the founder, of the Fukuoka Ichimonji school of Bizen. It is said that the Emperor conferred upon this school the right to inscribe the horizontal stroke forming the character *ichi* on their work to indicate that they were the Tenka Ichi, or 'The First Under Heaven'. It is not known to what extent the Emperor himself took part in the strenuous forging process, but it is likely that he would have himself heated and quenched the blades in the final *yakiire* hardening process. A number of *kiku gō saku* ('Imperial chrysanthemum works') are engraved on the tang with the chrysanthemum *mon* (badge) of the Japanese Imperial family, indicating that they were made by the former Emperor and his attendant smiths (no. 16). A number of these are in Ko Bizen style. The Emperor's interest must have considerably enhanced the prestige of the sword as an art object during a period when its efficacy as a weapon must have been the first requirement for the samurai of Kamakura.

Middle

Some few decades into the thirteenth century saw a further development in the shape of the sword blade, in keeping with the martial spirit at Kamakura, which had become quite removed from the culture of Kyoto. The Hōjō reinforced the traditions of strict military training by specifying in a legal code of 1232 the samurai's duty to devote himself to the study of horsemanship, archery and swordplay. Swordsmiths came to Kamakura to work, like the illustrious Kunitsuna of the Awataguchi group who was summoned from Kyoto by Hōjō Tokiyori in 1249. Others included Saburō Kunimune and Sukezane from Bizen.

Whereas the blades of the Heian and early Kamakura period were deeply curved at the base, slightly curved at the upper part and narrowed towards the point considerably, those of the middle Kamakura period were altogether broader, with little reduction in breadth over the length of the blade. This new type also had a deeper curve throughout their length. Perhaps due to an innate conservatism among swordsmiths that rebelled at the demand for such a change, the length of the kissaki remained unchanged, so that the points appear short and stubby. They are called *ikubi* ('bull-necked') kissaki, and are an important indicator for dating swords of this period.

The blades are altogether more robust, reflecting the growing importance of swordplay in combat between armoured protagonists. The *hira*, or flat, part of early tachi, was a simple plain surface, but at this time swords were made with a slightly convex section in order to cut through armour more effectively. This is known as *hamaguri ba*, or 'clam blade'.

Ken-type blades and hira zukuri tantō were made in this period. The tantō are invariably slender with a slight uchi zori and about 25 cm long. A number of new blade shapes, like *kammuri otoshi* ('crown drop') and *u-no-kubi* ('cormorant's neck'), are found, particularly on Yamato school work. The earliest existing signed naginata date from this time.

This was the golden age of Bizen swords. The Ichimonji schools flourished, producing swords with grandiose hamon with large forms of chōji known as *jūka* ('banked') chōji or *kawazu no ko* ('tadpole') chōji which on some swords extended almost up to the shinogi (no. 20). In the latter part of the thirteenth century branches of the Ichimonji moved from Fukuoka to Yoshioka, and to Katayama in neighbouring Bitchū Province. The hamon on Bizen swords was predominantly in nioi, in contrast to the konie of the early Bizen smiths, with vivid utsuri.

In the village of Osafune, known as the village of swordsmiths, Mitsutada and Nagamitsu forged fine-grained work with hamon of chōji softening out around the upper part of the blade, and with rolling continuous utsuri reflecting the chōji hamon. The work of the three smiths Mitsutada, his son or apprentice Nagamitsu and Sanenaga is characterised by a slight inward swell, or *midare komi*, in the boshi. These three smiths are known as Bizen *sansaku*, 'the three makers', and their boshi is called the sansaku boshi. In nearby Hatakeda Moriie and his school made swords in Osafune style.

Rai Kuniyuki and Kunitoshi of the Yamashiro school also made blades with chōji, yet not so flamboyant as the work of Bizen, and in konie contrasting with the essential nioi of Bizen blades. Chōji hamon appeared, in fact, on swords of many schools, like the Aoe of Bitchū Province. Smiths of the Awataguchi group, also of Yamashiro, who had provided several gō ban kaji (see p. 39), made blades with the finest clear jigane. Prominent among them was Yoshimitsu, who made tantō with suguha hamon and delicately rounded boshi (no. 18).

Although little is known of the smiths of Yamato (around the old capital Nara) during the Heian and early Kamakura periods, the work of several schools associated with temples at this time are clearly in the Yamato tradition. They were the Hōshō, the Taema named after Taema Temple, the Shikkake, the Senshuin, named after an extramural residence belonging to the Kōfukuji Temple, and the Tegai associated with the Tengai gate to the Tōdaiji Temple. Yamato school blades are more subdued than those of the Bizen smiths, probably reflecting their monastic connections, for they must have worked during the Heian period to equip the armies of *sōhei*, or warrior monks, in and around Nara. Probably for the same reason their early works are unsigned and therefore not easily identifiable. Their forging grain is basically masame, although more often a flowing itame, with jinie. However, masame in its pure form is found on some swords in almost perfectly parallel lines, particularly those of the Hōshō group. Their hamon is predominantly suguha in rich nie with variations including nijuba. The boshi is often *yakitsume* (ending at the back of the sword with no return), or *hakikake* ('brushed' – formed of a number of lines).

Late

In the eleventh year of the Bunei era, 1274, Kublai Khan's army attempted invasion of Japan with an armada of 900 ships. Prior to this a number of overtures from the Mongols had been rejected, and their envoys ill-treated. As news of the landing was heard, the Japanese gathered and sped to meet their enemy, eager for battle and glory; but the mounted samurai met an unexpectedly well-organised army little concerned with the niceties of Japanese battle etiquette. Moreover, the Mongol army was equipped with explosive weapons, unknown to the Japanese.

The Mongols met the Japanese with volleys of arrows from archers on foot, advancing to the sound of explosives and cymbals and terrifying the Japanese horses. Ranks of spearmen played havoc with the Japanese before the awesome long swords could be brought into play. Things might have gone badly for the Japanese but for a sudden storm which wrecked the Mongol fleet and destroyed a great part of the army who were at the time retired to their ships. Seven years later Kublai Khan came again with a greater army than before, to be met by Hōjō Tokimune at the head of an outnumbered army. Again the 'divine wind', or *shimpu*, commonly called *kamikaze*, blew and destroyed the second armada.

The experiences of fighting the Mongols no doubt contributed greatly to the sudden change in style of combat and military thinking, for the Japanese remained prepared for further invasion attempts throughout the ensuing half century.

During the late thirteenth century swords became longer than before, and in addition to the deeply curved koshi zori blades there were now swords of even curve more suited to infantry combat. These longer swords were of more even breadth throughout their length. The value of naginata and *yari* ('spears') was appreciated from the experiences against the Mongols, as was the vulnerability of horses to organised ranks of infantry. In addition to the uchi zori-curve daggers, straight-bladed weapons were made.

The defect of the ikubi kissaki was that the point was not suitable for thrusting into armour. If the edge of the kissaki became chipped, it might not always be possible to reshape it and still retain the hard edge portion. In addition, grooves carved along the shinogi ji in order to lighten the earlier blades usually extended past the yokote line, rendering it all the more difficult to reshape a broken point. From this period the kissaki was accordingly made longer, and the grooves stopped slightly lower down the blade.

At Kamakura Shintōgo Kunimitsu firmly established the Sōshū tradition. His name is often linked with that of Kunitsuna and Kunimune, and the *Kanchiin Bon* (see p. 13) contains two different lineages indicating on one that he studied under Sukezane, and on the other that he studied under Kunimune. His known swords with inscribed dates show that he was active at least between 1293 and 1334. Kunimitsu's hamon are suguha in nie. His jihada is rich in jinie, with swirling itame forming kinsuji at the hamon. Among his pupils were two of the most famous names

among Japanese swordsmiths – Yukimitsu and Masamune (nos 24, 25, 56).

Masamune had enormous influence on swordmaking throughout the country. His work and that of his school is characterised by nie, and particularly by jinie. The jigane is complex, formed by forging together different kinds of steels somehow to give improved strength and hardness. The effect is seen in the varied hues in the jihada of the swords. Masamune's blades are rich in jinie activity, with both bright and dark pools of chikei. The hamon is predominantly *notare* ('undulating') with midareba, deep and intense with varied lines of inazuma, sunagashi and kinsuji. The effect is not unlike the work of Yasutsuna of Hōki (no. 10) in its extremes of activity, and it is thought that Masamune may have consciously emulated him.

Sword-fittings

Black-lacquered and leather mountings remained in widespread use on the battlefield throughout the Kamakura period, but a more decorative type had evolved around the end of the Heian period. This was the *hyōgo kusari* ('military chained') tachi which was suspended by chains from the belt rather than by silk braid or leather straps (no. 21). These tachi have lacquered scabbards, sometimes covered with metal, and often with metal reinforcing strips along the back and edge and continuing on the hilt. Their tsuba are metal and decorated with free and imaginative designs.

Although the hyōgo kusari tachi was originally meant for combat, it survived during the second half of the Kamakura period as a votive offering to shrines and temples. In addition to no. 21, an example in the Tokyo National Museum which was given to the Mishina Taisha Shrine by the Uesugi family is sculpted roundly with flying birds on all the metalwork, and further decorated in high-relief gold-lacquer sculpture on the scabbard. Another in the Atsuta Shrine is decorated with the encircled cranes motif which appears on metalwork of the Momoyama and Edo periods (no. 93). Yet another example in the Sanage Shrine has *onagadori* ('long-tailed birds') carved roundly in relief and pierced on the *seppa* (metal spacers which sandwich the tsuba). All these pieces signify a decorative taste far removed from the Chinese-style kazari tachi.

In addition to tachi, naginata and tantō were made, but their mountings do not survive.

Horimono

Like those of the Heian period, horimono of the Kamakura period indicate the religious beliefs of the smiths, although it is not unlikely that the subjects were commissioned by their clients. The early subjects, Fudō Myō-Ō, dragons, kurikara, ken, *gomabashi* (ritual tongs) are all associated with the Shingon sect of Buddhism. The gomabashi motif was used together with a stylised lotus throne, *rendai*, a *kuwagata*, or 'hoe shape', the rope of Fudō Myō-Ō and Sanskrit.

Around the end of the Kamakura period the Shintō deity Hachiman, recognised as the god of archers, is represented on blades usually in the form of an invocation to his Bodhisattva aspect carved in Chinese characters or in Sanskrit. At this time horimono became somewhat longer, and might be arranged in rows along the blade.

Armour

The first ōyoroi of the Heian period was worn with a hoshi kabuto. Then the *suji* kabuto, made from vertical plates turned up along one side to form vertical ridges (suji) running from the base to the top of the helmet, was devised and became fashionable during the Kamakura period. At the same time, the change in emphasis from hand-to-hand horseback combat with the bow as the main weapon to close fighting between large numbers of warriors resulted in the need for more freedom of movement and correspondingly lighter armour.

---

16 Tachi blade

Kamakura period, 13th century
Inscribed with chrysanthemum mon; made by cloistered Emperor Go Toba and attendant smiths
L. 75.8 cm
Tokyo National Museum

The blade is in typical late Heian–early Kamakura style, with a deep koshi zori, fumbari and blade gently narrowing to a small kissaki. A single bohi on either side runs from above the mitsugashira down through the tang. The jigane is close-packed small itame with midare utsuri. The hamon is midare with large chōji, ashi and yō, and in konie. The boshi is slightly midare komi, ending in a small round return.

Swords bearing the imperial chrysanthemum indicating that Go Toba was involved in their manufacture are usually in Bizen, Bitchū or Yamashiro tradition depending on which of the gō ban kaji (p. 39) was in attendance. They are said to have been given as presents to the warriors of the north and west who had supported Go Toba in his campaigns to regain the throne. This blade has the characteristics of the early Ichimonji school of Bizen.

The sword was given to the Showa Emperor (reigned 1926–89) before his enthronement. The present mounting dates from the Momoyama period (see no. 68).

17 Tachi blade *(illus. on p. 44)*

Kamakura period, 13th century; Awataguchi group, Yamashiro school
Signed: Kunitomo
L. 74.2 cm
Sword Museum, Tokyo

This blade is of late Heian period shape which continued for some decades into the thirteenth century. It has koshi zori and fumbari and decreases in width towards the kissaki, which is slightly longer than typical Heian period pieces. It is decorated with a *koshihi* ('short waist groove') either side of the blade, and the tang is in its original *kijimata* ('pheasant's thigh') shape. The jigane is bright, formed of small itame with fine jinie, characteristic of Yamashiro work. The hamon is a narrow suguha in small nie with small midare, ashi, yō and kinsuji. The boshi has an elegant komaru.

Kunitomo's brothers, Hisakuni, Kuniyasu, Arikuni and Kunitsuna, were all excellent smiths. Hisakuni and Kuniyasu, together with Kunitomo, were numbered among the attendant smiths of Go Toba In (p. 39, no. 16). Their descendants included the great maker of tantō, Toshiro Yoshimitsu (no. 18).

18 Mōri Toshirō *(illus. on p. 45)*

Mid-Kamakura period, 13th century; Awataguchi group of Kyoto, Yamashiro school
Signed: Yoshimitsu
L. 26.5 cm
Tokyo National Museum, Important Cultural Property

This is a hira zukuri, uchi zori tantō – an elegant weapon with koitame grain, rather flowing towards the mune, and rich in jinie overall. The hamon is fine suguha with small midare and gunome, having ashi, in konie and with kinsuji. The carving on one side is gomabashi, and on the other a koshihi and soehi which are of *kakinagashi* type (narrowing through to the end of the tang). The boshi is komaru and hakikake. There are two mekugi ana, with the finely chiselled two-character signature starting just below the centre of the second hole, so that the top of the character *yoshi* is cut away.

This is the Mōri Toshiro referred to in the *Kyōhō Meibutsu Chō*. Many swords by Yoshimitsu have gomabashi, like the Okayama Toshiro, Masuda Toshiro and Shūmei Toshiro. This dagger was beloved by Mōri Terumoto, to whom it was given by Tokugawa Ieyasu. It was later given to Ikeda Mitsumasa, and in the fourteenth year of Meiji presented by the Ikeda family to the Emperor.

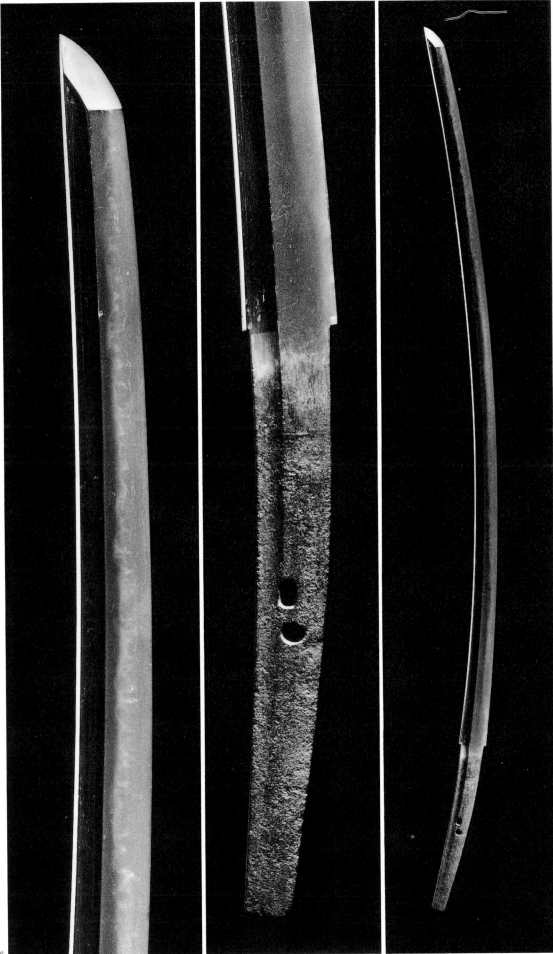

16

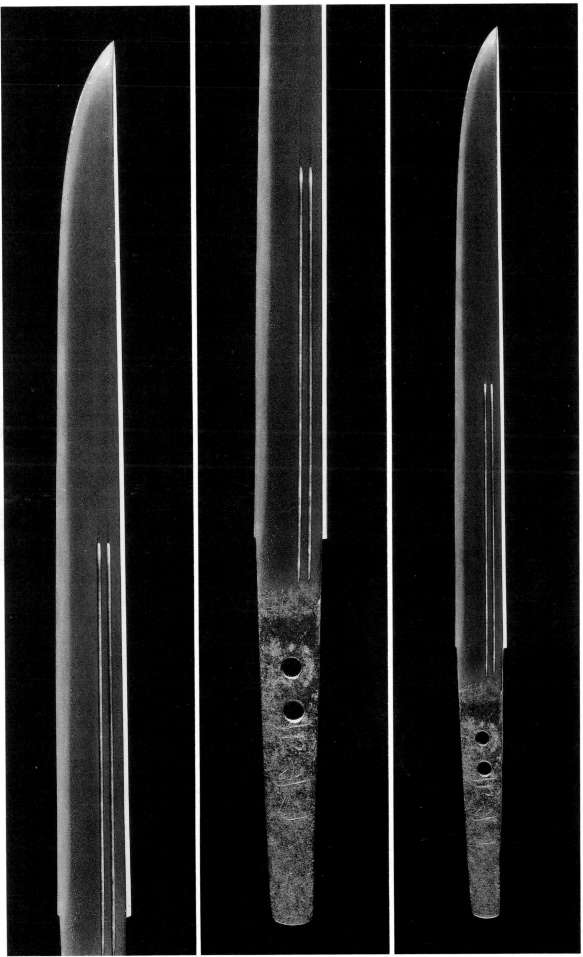

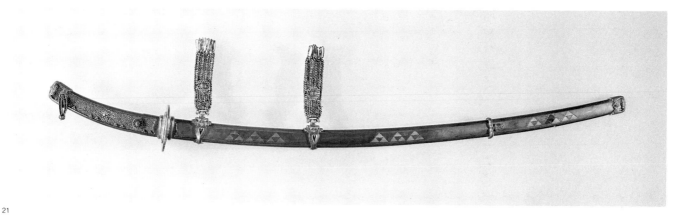

21

19 Tachi blade (illus. on p. 46)

Late Kamakura period, 13th century; Yamashiro
  school
Signed: Rai Kunimitsu
L. 80.6 cm
Tokyo National Museum, National Treasure

The jihida of this blade is koitame with some
flowing grain, often seen on work of the
Rai group, and much jinie. The hamon is a
broad suguha with small midare, ashi and
yō, rich in nie and settled. The boshi is the
most refined komaru. The blade, although
shortened about 15 cm, still retains its
signature. It is a heavy, wide and robust
blade, with no sign of wear. Its kissaki is of
the original bull-neck shape, like that of the
middle Kamakura period National Treasure
tachi by Ichimonji Yoshifusa (no. 20).

The Rai group flourished from the middle
Kamakura period in Kyoto together with
the Awataguchi group (see also no. 18).
Kunimitsu was one of the third generation
after the founder of the group, Kuniyuki,
and a contemporary of Rai Kunitsugu who
is thought to have studied under Masamune
at Kamakura.

20 Okadagiri (illus. on p. 47)

Middle Kamakura period, 13th century; Bizen
  Province, Ichimonji group
Signed: Yoshifusa
L. 69.1 cm
Tokyo National Museum, National Treasure

It is said that the Ichimonji ('the character
one') group of smiths was so named by the
retired swordmaking Emperor Go Toba,
implying that their work was the 'first' in
the world. This sword, designated a
National Treasure by the Japanese
government, must surely justify that
appellation.

Yoshifusa is representative of the
Fukuoka Ichimonji group, ranking together
with Sukezane and Norifusa. This sword is
of typical middle Kamakura period shape,
with a deep koshi zori curve, broad and of
even width with the characteristic stunted
ikubi kissaki. The jihada is a flowing close-
packed itame, with vivid midare utsuri. The
hamon is the most extravagant form of deep
nioi with jūka chōji and kawazu no ko chōji,
and abounding in ashi and yō.

The name Okadagiri ('Okada cutter')
derives from an episode during the battle
of Komaki Nagakute in 1584, when Oda
Nobukatsu used the sword to cut down and
kill a retainer, Okada Sukesaburō, whom he
believed to have been in secret
communication with Toyotomi Hideyoshi.

21 Hyōgo kusari tachi mounting

Kamakura period, 13th century
L. 105.0 cm
Tokyo National Museum, Important Cultural
  Property

The metal fittings are all plain polished
silver. The hilt is wrapped with white ray-
fish skin, and is pierced with a row of tawara
byō tang retainer pins (see no. 12) having
heads in the form of the triple fish-scale mon
of the Hōjō family. However, these are
purely decorative, and the blade is retained
by a mekugi which passes through silver-
gilt roundels also carrying the triple fish-
scale mon. At intervals the silver-covered
scabbard is engraved with the outlines of
the same mon, which is gilt. Few such early
pieces survive, and the many later dedicated
swords are either like this, with mounts
wholly covered in silver or gold, or with
ikakeji ('sprinkled with gold') lacquer
scabbards.

The mounting is contemporary with the
blade, which is a tachi of the Ichimonji
school (no. 22). These tachis were popular
gifts between warriors and the nobility
during the Heian and middle Kamakura
periods, but thereafter were given as
dedications to shrines and temples. This
example was given to Mishima Taisha
Shrine by the Hōjō clan in the Kamakura
period.

22 Tachi blade

Kamakura period, 13th century; Ichimonji school
L. 75.5 cm
Tokyo National Museum, Important Cultural
  Property

This blade belongs to the hyōgo kusari
mounting (no. 21), which follows its shape
exactly. The curve is a deep koshi zori which
continues along the tang. The small chōji
hamon and vivid utsuri are classic
characteristics of the early Ichimonji school.

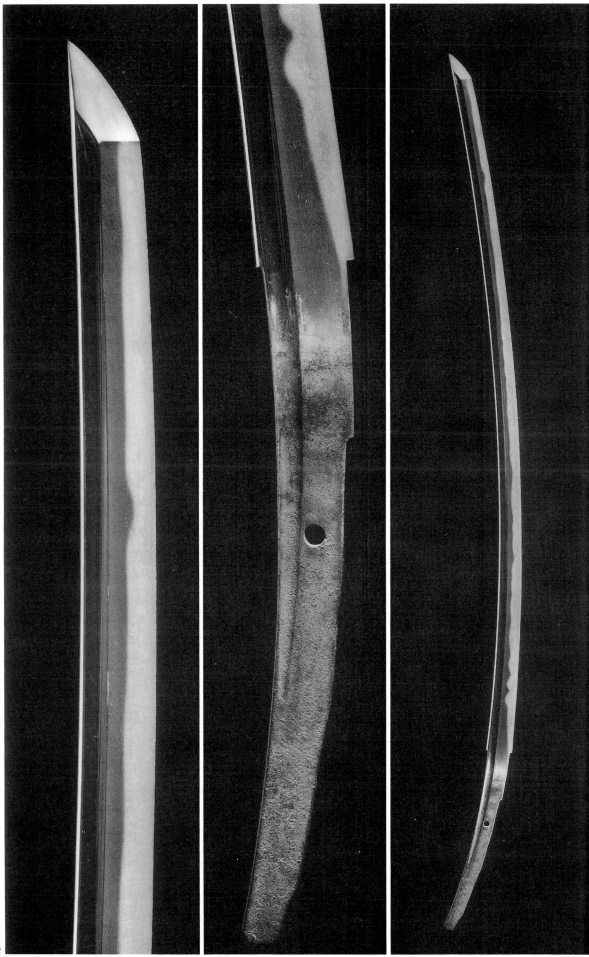

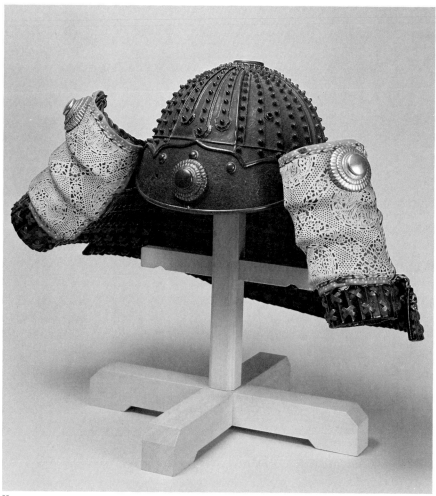

23

23 Helmet

Kamakura period, 13th century
H. (bowl) 9.4 cm
Sword Museum, Tokyo, Important Cultural
  Property.

The low hemispherical helmet-bowl shape
of the late Heian and early Kamakura period
developed into the elegant round *daienzan*
('great circular mountain') form of this typical
Kamakura period piece. It is composed of
twenty-eight plates, with twenty columns
of star-headed rivets from which the type
derives the name *hoshi kabuto*, or 'star
helmet'. The tehen no ana (see no. 15) is
4.9 cm in diameter, surrounded by a gilt-
copper *hachimanza* roundel which bears a
further small gilt star for each column on the
vertical plates. There is yet another star

below each row on the skirt of the bowl.
There are four sets of gilt rims covering the
turned-up *suji*, edges of the iron plates of
the bowl. The front of the bowl is decorated
with three decorative *shinogidare* strips, each
of which is three-layered, with gilded edges
and studded with further 'stars'. The peak
is characteristically almost vertical, and has
holes where there was once a fitting for
kuwagata. There are stylised
chrysanthemum decorations on the centre of
the peak and on both fukigaeshi, although
the original piece on the peak, together with
much of the copper rimming, has lost most
of its gilding. The shikoro is deep angled
with large leather-covered fukigaeshi set
well forward to provide ample protection
from the oblique front.

24 Ishida Masamune

Kamakura period, early 14th century
Unsigned; work of Masamune of Sōshū Province
L. 63.8 cm
Agency for Cultural Affairs, Tokyo, Important
  Cultural Property

Perhaps highest prized among the daimyō
of the Muromachi and Edo periods was the
work of Masamune, whose name has
become synonymous with the
establishment of the Sōshū school in the late
Kamakura period. Like this blade,
Masamune's tachi were of such great length
that they have been cut down to a
convenient size for wearing in uchigatana
mountings, and have therefore lost the
inscriptions which were on the original
tangs. However, a number of signed tantō
survive which are demonstrably by the same
hand.

This sword has a number of battle marks,
two on the mune, three on the flat of the
blade and one on the tang. This last must
have been sustained before the sword was
shortened in the Muromachi period. The
grain is close packed itame with fine jinie
and liberal patches of chikei. The hamon is
overall notare with gunome midare and
some chōji, and contains bright varied lines
of kinsuji, sunagashi and deep ashi. The
boshi is midare with a slight feeling of
hakikake at the return.

The sword is named after Ishida
Mitsunari, who is said either to have
received it directly from Toyotomi
Hideyoshi, or, according to the *Kyōhō
Meibutsu Chō*, to have been given it by
Ukita Hideie who bought it from Mori
Wakasa no Kami for 400 *kan* of gold. Ishida
Mitsunari had been close to Hideyoshi. He
achieved a peace treaty with Korea and
safely evacuated the Japanese invasion
forces while concealing the fact of
Hideyoshi's death. Several of the returning
daimyō, undoubtedly with the
understanding of Tokugawa Ieyasu, sought
to kill Ishida. However, he appealed directly
to Ieyasu for help, and Ieyasu instructed
Yuki Hideyasu, adopted son of Hideyoshi,
to provide him with an escort to his estate.
In gratitude, according to the *Meibutsu Chō*,
Ishida entrusted one of the Yuki clan
retainers with the sword as a gift for
Hideyasu. Mitsunari must have been intent
on a safe future for the blade with his own
future still in the balance. The story well
invokes the spirit of the warriors of the
Sengoku period.

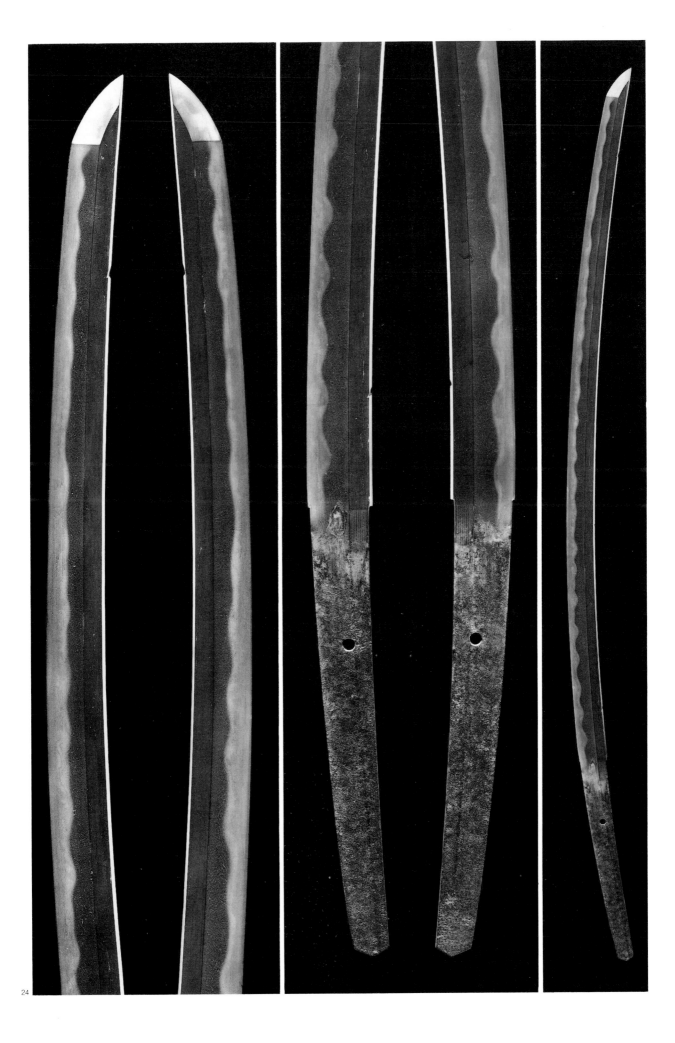

5

The Nambokuchō or Yoshino period

(1333–1392)

Sources of dissatisfaction with the Hōjō government included the fact that rewards and recompenses promised in return for services fighting and maintaining a state of readiness against the Mongols were not paid. The Hōjō lost control over distant provinces. Bickering among various factions eventually resulted in open war, and Kamakura was stormed in 1333 by forces representing the Emperor Godaigo, to fall after several days' fierce defence. The seat of power returned to Kyoto, but after only three years a *daimyō* ('provincial lord'), Ashikaga Takeuji, established a rival emperor in the north of Kyoto. Sixty years of civil war ensued, continual battles across the moors of Yoshino near Kyoto giving another name to the Nambokuchō ('Northern and Southern Courts') period. The whole country was in turmoil. Kyoto was ravaged time and time again. Swordmaking flourished. It was not until 1392 that Ashikaga Yoshimitsu emerged victorious, and the northern dynasty was confirmed.

Many swords with a cutting length of more than a metre, and sometimes much longer, were fashionable. These were eminently effective when fighting on foot against cavalry. They are sometimes called *nodachi* ('moor swords'), and as they were too long to carry at the belt they were often carried across the back, which gave them the name *seoi dachi* ('swords carried on the back'). These huge weapons were occasionally mounted in disposable scabbards or wrapped in paper or straw. Very few of these great blades have survived in their original length, since later generations cut them down to a convenient size for everyday wear, to the extent that the signatures have been lost. However, several votive offerings in temples and shrines remain as evidence of the immense proportions which were attained. One excellent blade, 180 cm long, by Tomoyuki of Bungo Province in the collection of Oyamazumi Shrine has been designated a National Treasure.

Daggers were broad and evenly curved, as were naginata, but most naginata of the time, like the nōdachi, have been cut down or converted into swords. Some daggers from this period have tangs with a pronounced slope and were possibly mounted as *mete zashi*, or 'horse-hand swords' carried on the right side of the waist with the cutting edge forward. The right hand was known as the 'horse hand' since traditionally the bow had been carried in the left. The dagger could be drawn and used to make upward cuts at the weak points under the armour of an opponent.

New provisional schools were formed by smiths who had been influenced by the Sōshū style. A number of smiths are thought to have studied under Masamune, to return to their home provinces in the wake of the fall of Kamakura. In the Edo period a list of ten pupils of Masamune was published, but there is no certain contemporary record. Closest in style to Masamune is Sadamune (no. 25), who is often described as his son. Sadamune worked from the late Kamakura and during the Nambokuchō period, but no signed pieces of his work are known. Akihiro and Hiromitsu made many broad daggers with a midare or *gunome* (abruptly undulating) midare hamon. Some of their swords have hamon which emerge all over the blade in patches and circles. This characteristic, known as *hitatsura*, is also found on the work of Hasebe Kunishige of Kyoto and smiths of later schools.

A smith of the Yamato Tegai group, Kaneuji, is said also to have been one of Masamune's pupils. He moved to Shizu in Mino Province, and with his several pupils established the last of the classic 'Five Traditions' (Bizen, Yamashiro, Yamato, Sōshu and Mino), the Mino school, which flourished during the Muromachi period. His swords have masame near the edge and at the shinogi, a feature which remained on later Mino work and was inherited by the first of the *shintō* (Momoyama and Edo period 'new swords') smiths.

In Osafune, Kanemitsu (no. 26), son of Kagemitsu, continued the Bizen tradition, making grand nōdachi first with gunome hamon in the old Bizen style and in later life sometimes with a swelling form of hamon called *notare*. Nagashige, or Chōgi, made very broad blades with large undulating hamon. Of all Masamune's pupils Gō Yoshihiro was closest in style to Yukimitsu (see p. 41). Although no signed blades by him exist, sword appraisers identify his work with the inlaid character *gō*, since he lived in Matsukura gō (gō meaning district) of Etchū Province; later writers and sword appraisers have used the characters for 'bay' and 'five', also pronounced gō, to describe him. Also of Etchū, Norishige made blades with a characteristic vivid itame hada with large irregular bands of alternate dark and bright steel, which has been called matsukawa ('pine bark') or *hijiki hada* (a form of edible seaweed). Norishige specialised in daggers with an uchi zori-type curve, rather more pronounced than that of the middle Kamakura period. Sa, or Saemon Saburō, another pupil of Masamune, took the Sōshū style to Chikushū. His school continued for several generations.

The last smiths of the Aoe school of Bitchū made large distinctive blades, both tachi and tantō. Many of them worked with a sloping form of chōji, known as *saka* chōji. Their jigane is bright, with a straight form of utsuri, or *bo utsuri*, which is found also on some Osafune work particularly of the Oei era (1394–1427).

Sword-fittings

Leather mountings continued to be used, especially for the long nōdachi, since they were weatherproof and rugged. Some tachi were provided with leather covers over the tsuba in order to keep rain out of the scabbard mouth. Two famous sword-mountings, the so-called Oni Maru and the Sasamaru are of this type, and have leather stretched over all the metal components. The Sasamaru mounting is said to have been carried by Ashikaga Takauji (1305–58), and is so named from the carving of *sasa* grasses on the tsuba. This sword is an early example of the *ito maki no tachi* type (tachi 'wrapped with cords'), which is bound with criss-crossed braid both on the hilt and on the upper part of the scabbard to protect it from damage when worn with armour.

A number of koshigatana mountings survive from this period. They are of the *aikuchi* ('meeting mouths') type which has no tsuba. Their hilts are often covered wholly with metal, pierced or carved with rich decoration, and the scabbards are often similarly clad with long metal wrappings (no. 27). These koshigatana are sometimes equipped with a *kōgai* which fits into a pocket in the scabbard. The kōgai is a kind of bodkin which might be used to dress the hair, and which has a small protrusion at the end said to be for cleaning the ears. The middle Edo period book *Bankin Sangyō Bukuro* ('A Bagful of Metal Industries') records that the kōgai was once used as an identification mark, to be left in the body of a fallen enemy in order to be able to claim the victory at a later time.

Uchigatana with tsuba carried through the belt with the edge uppermost are known from illustrations in scroll paintings to have existed from the Heian and Kamakura periods, although being carried by low-class soldiers they were probably of poor quality and have not survived. A fine example of the Nambokuchō period in the Kasuga Shrine is elegantly decorated with lozenges in makie lacquerwork, and has a fine-quality unsigned blade.

Horimono

Up to the late Kamakura period bohi-type grooves extended past the *mitsugashira*, the point where the yokote joins the shinogi, but this introduced difficulty in reshaping a point if it became broken (p. 41). The grooves of many of the long broad Nambokuchō period tachi typically stop a few centimetres below the mitsugashira. The horimono remain of religious significance, with many invocations to Shintō divinities in addition to the Shingon paraphernalia. Masamune had pierced gomabashi right through the broad-bladed tantō known as Hōchō ('kitchen knife') Masamune, thereby introducing something of a decorative element into the art of horimono, which was taken up by his pupils. Sadamune used Shintōgo Kunimitsu's gomabashi, kuwagata, rendai and Sanskrit to decorate throughout the length of the blades of his tantō, as did his pupil Nobukuni. In general horimono became larger and somewhat shallow carved. From this period onward there occur religious horimono in the lower part of the blade together with grooves starting higher up.

Armour

Two new types of armour were developed during the Kamakura and Nambokuchō periods, the *dōmaru* and the *haramaki*. At first these lighter armours were intended for the lower-grade infantry, but during the Nambokuchō period they became popular also with the high-ranking samurai.

The dōmaru hinged around the body fastening on the right side, but unlike the ōyoroi there was no waidate covering the join. There were several other differences between the new forms of armour and the ōyoroi. The tsurubashiri across the front was dispensed with, as were the two hanging breast pieces, the sendan no ita and the kyubi no ita, since the bow lost its position of importance during the Nambokuchō wars. They were replaced with similar, smaller, leaf-shaped *gyōyō* covering the suspension pieces in front of the shoulders. The kusazuri became divided into more hanging portions, typically seven or eight, laced looser together to facilitate moving around on foot. Many existing dōmaru were adopted during the Yoshino and Muromachi periods by high-ranking samurai, who kept the great helmets and ō sode of the days of the ōyoroi (no. 15).

The haramaki was similar to the dōmaru, basically also formed of linked kozane. It wrapped around the body to join at the back. The early Nambokuchō pieces are very small and light, providing protection only for the trunk, but like the dōmaru during the Yoshino and Muromachi period they came to be used with helmets and ō sode by men of rank.

25 Ishida Sadamune

Nambokuchō period, 14th century
Unsigned; attributed to Sadamune, Sōshū
    Province
L. 31.3 cm
Agency for Cultural Affairs, Tokyo, Important
    Cultural Property

This tantō blade is in the broad, long-pointed style with a low curve common to smiths of the Nambokuchō period, and especially to Sadamune's fellow Sōshū-tradition workers. The deeply sloping 'boat-shaped' tang is found on Sōshū work right through the Muromachi period.

The carvings on one side are of a stylised ken-type sword, with above its point a kuwagata, and above that a lotus throne and Sanskrit character. The other side of the blade carries the gomabashi and also a Sanskrit character. These religious motifs were used by Shintogo Kunimitsu, the founder of the Sōshū tradition, Masamune and later smiths of the school, especially Sadamune's pupil, Nobukuni of Kyoto.

The tantō exhibits all Sadamune's characteristics. The hamon is notare with gunome midare in nie, full of energetic kinsuji. The tight itame on the body carries a rich dispersal of jinie, with powerful lines of chikei. This sword, together with the Ishida Masamune (no. 24), was owned by the daimyō Ishida Mitsunari who was given it by Toyotomi Hideyoshi. (See also mounting, no. 83.)

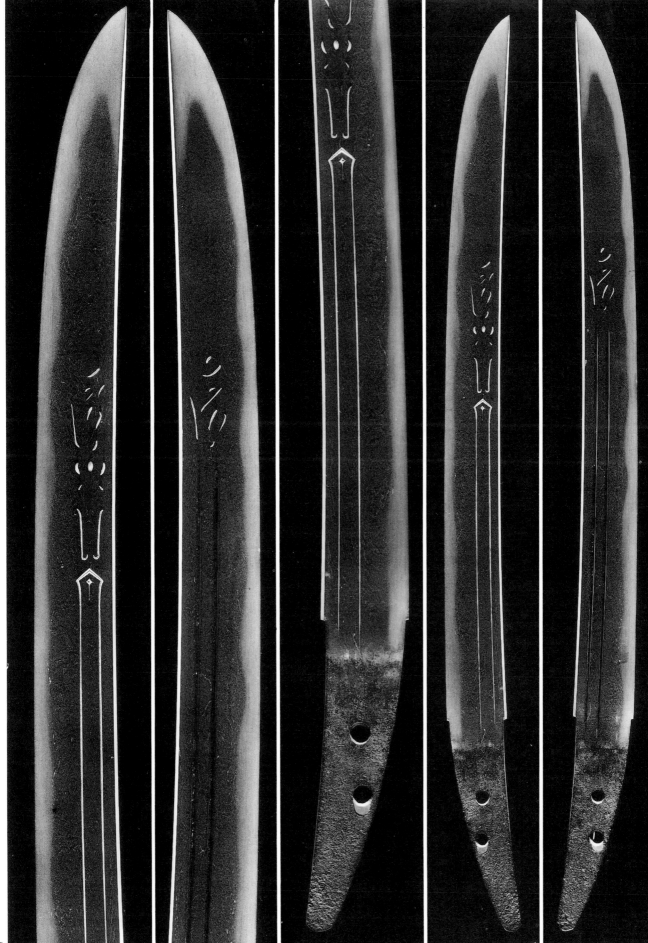

26 Tachi blade

Dated: Enbun Yonnen nigatsu hi (a day in February 1358)
Signed: Bizen Kuni Osafune Kanemitsu
L. 93 cm
Tokyo National Museum, Important Cultural Property

This blade has the massive proportions of a nodachi, broad, and with a shallow even curve and extended kissaki. The hamon is notare with gunome, clearly defined with konie. The jigane is fine koitame, with white midare utsuri. The heavy sword is lightened by two full-length grooves which pass right through the tang. Out of superstition the 'four' in the date inscription is interestingly written as a double-character two, avoiding the use of the standard form which can be pronounced *shi*, meaning 'death'. Kanemitsu was active over several decades, and some believe there were two generations.

27 Koshigatana mounting

(illus. in colour on p. 82)

Nambokuchō period, 14th century
L. (overall) 55 cm
Kyoto National Museum, Important Cultural Property

The hilt is formed of smooth polished silvered metal, with pierced gilt-copper peony decoration wrapped around it. The scabbard is made of the skin of a certain kind of ray-fish found in the South China sea, lacquered black and polished smooth to show the apparent plum motif. Ray-fish skin was used on scabbards for its durability as well as its decorative effect, although few examples of a mounting in such fine condition survive from this period. The blade which belongs to this mounting is an unsigned work of the Yamato Senshuin group, and the mounting is probably contemporary with it.

   This kind of mounting was known as a *koshigatana* ('waist sword') since it was carried at the waist, but later swords without tsuba became known as *aikuchi* ('meeting mouths'). Koshigatana mountings of the Nambokuchō period are often equipped with a pocket for a kozuka and sometimes also for a kōgai, and, like this piece, most have a small projection below the kurikata called a *kaeri tsuno*, whose purpose is to prevent the scabbard slipping upwards through the belt.

28

28 Haramaki

Nambokuchō period, 14th century
H. (cuirass) 63.6 cm
Tokyo National Museum

This *haramaki* ('trunk wrapping') is made of small iron kozane plates linked together with braid and covered with leather.

   Versions of the light haramaki were introduced during the Kamakura period, but together with the dōmaru they became popular with high-ranking warriors during the struggles between the rival courts in the Nambokuchō period. This armour is said to have been worn by a retainer of Tachibana Masanari named Onchi Sakon. There is a mark of a sword cut on one of the shoulder-pieces.

6

The Muromachi period

(1392–1573)

The Muromachi period is named after the area in Kyoto where Ashikaga Yoshimitsu set up his government following the unification of the country in 1393. During an initial period of peace the constructive spirit of the Kamakura period prevailed. The Ashikagas renewed trade and cultural links with China, Yoshimitsu himself adopting Chinese dress. This was a period of philosophical study, and particularly the pursuit of Zen Buddhism through the arts. Schools of kendō, the Nō theatre, Tea and *suibokuga* (ink painting) flourished under Ashikaga patronage.

However, inattention to the details of government, and arguments over succession, led the country yet again into civil war in 1439. The Ōnin rebellion in 1467 signalled a century of discord giving name to the Sengoku Jidai, or 'The Age of Warring Provinces'. Central government became impossible, and the provincial lords ruled their own lands independently. Inter-clan warfare was fought largely by great armies of foot soldiers, or *ashigaru* ('light foot'), armed with spears and swords. The situation might have continued had not firearms been inadvertently delivered into the hands of the Japanese when a Portuguese vessel was grounded on an island called Tanegashima in 1543. The skills of the swordsmith found ready application in the manufacture of guns, all in strict imitation of the matchlock guns recovered from the ship and of superlative quality. It was with 3,000 such guns that in 1575 Oda Nobunaga obtained a decisive victory over his enemy, Takeda Katsuyori, at the battle of Nagashino. The advent of the firearm signalled the end of the traditional savage hand-to-hand warfare, and heralded some peace and stability to the nation. Nobunaga made the centre of government at Momoyama, in Kyoto, raising one of the new generation of huge stone castles erected to protect the daimyō against assault by firearms. After the death of Nobunaga, followed by that of Toyotomi Hideyoshi, his immediate successor, Tokugawa Ieyasu became Shogun. Ieyasu made his home at Edo, present-day Tokyo, and improved the fortifications there to build a castle, the walls of which now encompass the Imperial palace. The position of the Tokugawa clan was consolidated in 1625, after the supporters of Hideyoshi's son were defeated following a siege of Osaka Castle, and the family ruled as Shoguns in Edo for over two and a half centuries until the restoration to Imperial rule in 1867.

In the early part of the period a number of smiths made tachi in style similar to those of the middle Kamakura period. But the change in emphasis from cavalry to infantry led to the introduction of the uchigatana, a somewhat shorter sword which was carried thrust through the belt with the edge uppermost. Tachi were signed on the side of the tang facing outwards when worn. The same convention applied to uchigatana, so that they are signed on the opposite side of the tang. Typically, both tachi and uchigatana of the period are deeply curved in the upper part of the blade – the so-called *saki zori* curve. This is considered to increase cutting efficiency and to facilitate drawing the weapon. On many swords there is little or no curve at the base of the blade, the shinogi line continuing straight into the tang.

The same saki zori curve is evident on naginata of the period, which, while generally shorter than those of the Nambokuchō period, typically swell out broadly at the striking part, the *monouchi*. Yari were used like naginata for both cutting and thrusting. Their blades varied from just a few centimetres to over 60 cm in length. Most were around 7 or 8 cm long, and either of small triangular or diamond-shaped cross-section. There were also leaf-shaped blades, *jūmonji* yari, which had two shorter cross blades at the base, or the *katakama* yari, with a single perpendicular additional blade. A number of exotic variations are found with combinations of different-shaped blades. In general yari of the Muromachi period can be distinguished from later work by the greater length of the neck between the tang and the start of the sharp edge.

Some swords were made with the shinogi portion of the blade narrowing towards the *mune* (back), so that the cross-section of the blade is a flattened diamond shape. This *oroshi* mune construction lightened the blade and was no doubt thought to reduce friction during the cut. Many short uchigatana, around 60 cm in length, were made. Some straight daggers were produced, as well as slightly curved hira zukuri-type weapons around 30 cm long. The short, slightly curved, double-edged, or *moroha zukuri*, dagger was introduced, extending further the range of cuts which could be inflicted at close quarters, previously the preserve of the mete zashi. Some daggers were of the complex u-no-kubi or kammuri otoshi shapes, found previously on Yamato school work of the middle Kamakura period. A class of dagger known as a *yoroi doshi* ('armour piercer'), which must have originated during the Kamakura period, thick and narrowing towards the point, is also found; but probably the most marked innovation was the introducion of the *wakizashi*, or 'side sword'. This was a short weapon similar in shape to the uchigatana, usually well under 60 cm in length. It must have fallen naturally to the ashigaru to carry such a sword in addition to their spears. Samurai also took to wearing a pair of swords – uchigatana and wakizashi – the wakizashi to be carried at all times and the uchigatana also when out on business. By the end of the Muromachi period such pairs of swords, or *daishō* ('great and small'), had become virtually standard dress. Luxurious matched mountings were made for the wealthy samurai.

Although many excellent smiths worked during the Muromachi period, vast numbers of inferior blades were made to satisfy the increased demand for weapons for the ashigaru. The smiths of Mino and Bizen virtually mass-produced serviceable blades of little artistic merit. These were called *sokutō* ('bundled swords') and *kazu uchi mono* ('things made in number'), and they were often inscribed falsely with the names of well-known smiths. An example of this practice is documented in the *Kakitsuki* chronicle, the record of the era 1441–3. Akamatsu Mitsuke of Buzen Province ordered 300 swords to be made by Yasumitsu, who was one of the foremost of the smiths of Osafune village in Bizen Province. This would have represented a lifetime's work for Yasumitsu, but the order was probably fulfilled in a short space of time. Naturally, the poorer of these kazu uchi mono have not survived, but there are in existence many quite serviceable swords whose only real failing is bearing a fake signature.

Bizen remained for most of the Muromachi period a centre for sword manufacture. At first smiths like Yasumitsu and Morimitsu made excellent swords in the old style, with gunome chōji or suguha with utsuri. The utsuri of these Ōei Bizen blades is often straight, or bo utsuri, in contrast to the chōji or midare utsuri of the Kamakura period. Later, examples can be found of suguha along half the blade, and gunome or other violent activity along the remainder of the blade. The traditional utsuri disappears by the mid-Muromachi period, and nie becomes predominant on blades in place of the nioi which had previously marked standard Bizen ware. At Osafune some smiths, like Sukesada and Katsumitsu, made excellent blades with characteristic hamon full of movement but which cannot match the subtlety of Kamakura period work. Instead of pure gunome there occur complex formations, with the gunome breaking away at the heads and valleys, forming structures like the *kani no tsume* ('crab's claws') found on the work of Sukesada. Many of the Sue Bizen swords (late Bizen work of the Sengoku period) had suguha hamon, and these characteristically contain yō within the hardened portion. The Sōshū tradition continued, with smiths like those of the Shitahara group producing blades with large midare hamon in nie. Their hitatsura hamon introduced in the Nambokuchō period now appeared on works of other schools, including the great producers of Bizen and Mino.

The Mino tradition had broadened since the days of Saburō Kaneuji. Many smiths, using the character *kane* as part of their name, forged practicable blades. Kaneuji's slightly pointed effect in the hamon developed into geometrical patterns like the *sambon sugi* ('three cryptomerias') pattern used by Kanemoto. Kanefusa popularised the large, roundly undulating gunome hamon, sometimes called 'priest's head' gunome. Kanetsune, Kanesada, Kaneyoshi and others specialised in suguha, distinguishable from the work of other schools by *fushi*, or 'thickets', at intervals along the hamon. Kanesada made large gunome hamon, called *hako* ('box') gunome, or *uma no ha* ('horse teeth' gunome). A round protruding Jizō boshi, named after the shaven head of the Bodhisattva Jizō, is an easily recognisable Mino characteristic. A feature of all late Muromachi, especially that of Bizen, Seki and Sōshū, work is a deep return of the boshi. Other smiths, like Sukesada and Sukemitsu of Bizen, or Kanesada of Seki in Mino, made so-called *ichimai* boshi which filled the kissaki region.

Of the many skilled individual smiths Muramasa of Ise (no. 33) deserves particular mention. His work contains much of both Sōshū and Mino traditions. Muramasa's jigane is often whitish, like the work of Kanesada and other good Mino smiths. His hamon varied considerably and included notare, gunome, and his own particular variant of sambon sugi. Muramasa's swords have acquired a certain notoriety, since they are said to have caused injury or death to several members of the Tokugawa family.

A number of groups continued to work in their old provinces in Kyūshū. Of them the most prolific were the Takada group of Bungo Province, where swordmaking had flourished since the time of Yukihira, the Heian period master.

Sword-fittings

Although tachi were still made during the early Muromachi period, the uchigatana quickly gained in popularity with all classes of swordsmen. The scabbards of the uchigatana were of lacquered wood, and usually only the hilt fittings were metal. The scabbard was equipped with a *kurikata* protrusion with a hole through it to carry a *sageo* cord used to secure the weapon in the belt. A few centimetres below the kurikata was a *kaeri tsuno* ('return horn') which served to prevent the sword from rising in the belt.

The small metal fittings in the early period were usually of yamagane, either gilt, patinated or lacquered over. The decorative techniques included openwork, line engraving, a surface texture formed with a hollow punch producing an effect like fish roe called *nanako*, and inlay of dissimilar metals. From around the end of the Nambokuchō period a black patinated alloy of copper with from one to five per cent gold, called *shakudō*, was used.

Among the tachi *kanagushi*, the makers of metal fittings for scabbards and hilts, was Gotō Yūjō (1440–1512), who had been schooled in the Mino tradition using predominantly Chinese-style designs. He was a skilled metallurgist and specialised in working with shakudō of his own composition. Yūjō was retained by Ashikaga Yoshimasa, for whom he made *midokoromono* for uchigatana mountings. Midokoromono (literally 'things in three places') consisted of the small menuki ornaments placed either side of the hilt under the binding, the *kozuka* (hilt of the utility knife kept in a pocket in the scabbard) and the kōgai (see p. 53). Yūjō's forte was minute repoussé work, either in gold or shakudō with details in gold inlay. His designs were of the Chinese themes beloved of the Ashikaga Shoguns.

The Gotō family continued to serve the Ashikagas, and later the Tokugawas through seventeen generations. As a most trusted servant of the government, one of the family, Kōjō, controlled the manufacture of money at the *kinza*, or mint, making the gold coins or *ōban* of the Tenshō era (1573–92). The first four generations did not sign their works, but many were later appraised by their descendants. Among such are menuki made by the earliest generations which have been mounted at some later date on to kozuka or kōgai.

In addition to the highly decorative gilt metal fittings there were, of course, more sombre pieces, often in iron. Russet or black patinated iron resists corrosion and possesses a subdued beauty which was highly valued by the samurai. Iron, in particular, was used to make the most important part of the whole mounting, the tsuba. Distinct styles of tsuba for uchigatana mountings by specialist makers are recognisable from around the early Muromachi period. An early type of thin iron plate work with the minimum of design is identified with the work of armour makers, while rather more robust pieces are often said to be swordsmiths' work. These iron plate tsuba with their simple pierced designs are interesting reminders of Muromachi period taste, expressing the religious, philosophical or poetic concepts of the samurai. This type of pierced design is called *kage sukashi*, or 'negative silhouette', where the iron is cut away leaving the pierced shape of the desired motif. In *yō sukashi*, or 'positive silhouette' work, the ground is cut away to leave iron in the shape of the motif. The decorative potential of both techniques was extended during the Edo period to include a greater variety of subject-matter. The contrast between the rich variety in the texture of dark iron and the startling effect of the cut-away portions gives an effect not dissimilar to *sumi* ink painting.

Other Muromachi types of tsuba include Ōnin tsuba, associated with the Ōnin era (1466–77). They are thin iron plates, sometimes pierced with a design in kage sukashi and inlaid with arrays of brass dots. *Kamakura bori* tsuba were carved in relief with pictures of flowers, birds and landscapes, in particular those containing temple buildings. The Shōami school continued through the Muromachi and Edo periods. Some of their early work includes pierced tsuba with brass inlay. Kaneie of Fushimi (no. 65) carved free pictorial designs in high relief, which resemble ink paintings, seemingly unbounded by the restrictions in size and shape of the tsuba.

Owari Province produced a long tradition of pierced iron tsuba in yō sukashi. The rims of work of the school are characteristically thick, and the thickness of the plate decreases towards the centre *seppa dai* portion which carries the hole through which the blade passes. The colour and feel of Owari iron is deep and rich, and the surface has a grainy appearance called *tekkotsu* which results from the forging process. Similar tsuba were made at Kanayama, a village at the north of Atta in Owari. Kanayama work tends to be more vigorous than Owari pieces, although the dimensions are overall smaller.

Also related to Owari work are the later Yagyū tsuba, made to the liking of the swordsman Yagyū Renyasai Toshikane (1625–94), of the Shinkage Ryū school of kendō, who was retained by the Tokugawas in Owari.

In Kyoto elegant themes were expressed in work known as Kyō sukashi, pierced work with rather rounded designs, similarly in positive silhouette. The themes are often taken from nature, frequently containing flowers and insects, and the work is more pictorial than the stylised Owari pieces. Kyō sukashi tsuba are usually round, with flat surfaces and delicately carved. The hole for the blade is usually narrow and elongated. The style continued from the Muromachi through the Edo period. Earlier pieces have been called Heianjō sukashi.

Horimono

Further deities were carved on the blades of the Muromachi period, for many swordsmiths were devotees of the mystic sects, half Shintō and half Buddhist, like the Gassan group of Dewa Province who were adherents of the Shugendō sect of mountain worshippers. The *sansha* ('three shrines') belief in the three Shintō deities of either Hachiman or Hie Gōgongen, guardian deity of Hiezan, or Kasuga Daimyōjin or Utsunomiya Daimyōjin centred on Tenshōno Daijin (Amaterasu) was widespread. The names of these deities are found engraved on sword tangs.

Around the end of the sixteenth century Daikoku Ten appears in armour, in his guise as a Buddhist guardian. He is found especially on the work of Kunihirō, Daidō of Mino and Muramasa. The Niō guardian kings, Tōtō Tenjin, the deity of learning, and figures of the Shitennō religion, Marishi Ten and Tamonten, are also found. Military mottoes occur sometimes engraved on the tangs.

From the end of the Muromachi period specialist sculptors emerged to decorate swords made by others.

Armour

Dōmaru and haramaki continued to be used by all ranks of warriors. With the Sengoku period the authority of the ruling samurai somewhat declined. The outcome of battle was often decided by group tactics using common spearmen. The lower ranks often had to be content with the most meagre protection, usually a *hara ate*, or breastplate, which covered just the front and sides of the trunk, secured by leather or textile straps across the back. The ashigaru might also wear a *jingasa*, a shallow conical hat which was sometimes of iron. The increasing use of spear formations, as well as the introduction of the gun after 1543, rendered traditional fine-quality armour and the bow almost obsolete. The bow being superseded by the gun, there was no longer a need for the ō sode, although small versions were retained. For the same reason the large fukigaeshi on the helmet were gradually dispensed with, although small versions remained to bear family mon. Further protective pieces were added, like the *seita*, a loose vertical plate of linked kozane which covered the join down the back of the haramaki, and a split armoured apron, or *haidate*, which hung under the kusazuri to protect low over the knees. Different types of lighter suneate were made of vertical plates linked with mail. In addition to the *happuri* type of cover for forehead and cheeks, which had been used since the Kamakura period, russet or lacquered iron *hoate* ('cheek pieces'), which covered just the lower half, and full masks, which covered the whole face, became popular. The *nodowa*, a flexible gorget, was introduced, even though the mask itself might have a hanging *tare* which covered the throat.

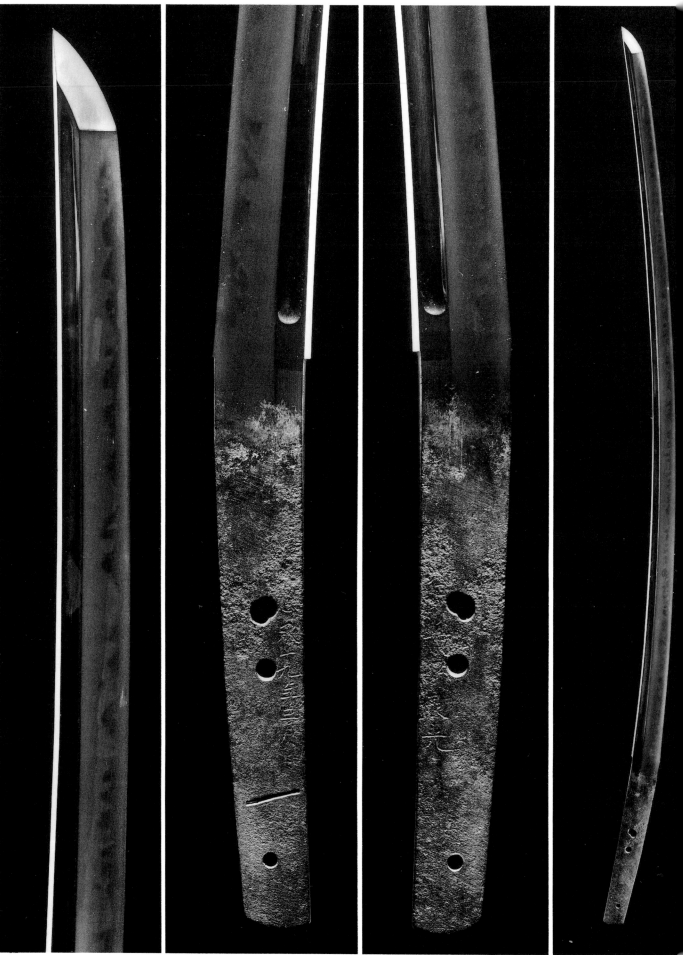

29 Tachi blade

Dated: Ōei Jukyunen sangatsu hi (a day in March
    1412)
Signed: Bishū Osafune Yasumitsu ('Yasumitsu of
    Osafune village in Bishū Province')
L. 74.6 cm
Sword Museum, Tokyo

This robust blade has the koshi zori curve
of the Kamakura period, but with a
pronounced saki zori curve which marks
Muromachi period blades. The jigane is
vivid, consisting of itame with mokume, and
jinie with chikei and patches of jifu utsuri.
The hamon is of large and open gunome
mixed with chōji, predominantly in nioi but
with nie and some sunagashi. Yasumitsu,
together with Morimitsu of Osafune, are
representative of the early Muromachi
period Bizen school, the Ōei Bizen (Ōei era,
1394–1427) smiths. Their work is in
conscious revival of the blade patterns of
the Osafune and Ichimonji schools of the
Kamakura period, but unlike the pure chōji
of their predecessors, the Ōei Bizen smiths
produced a complex of chōji and gunome
together. They also made wakizashi blades
with the same abrupt saki zori curve as on
their long swords.

30 Yari

Muromachi period, 15th century; Mino Province
Signed: Senshuin saku ('made by Senshuin')
L. (blade) 62.5 cm

Large yari of this type, with a shinogi either
side of the blade, appeared around the mid-
Muromachi period, although most weapons
of the time had shorter poor-quality blades
for the armies of ashigaru. The jigane is a
flowing form of itame which transforms to
masame in places. The hamon is small
gunome with chōji and midare in small nie,
and with minute pointed formations, many
small ashi, faint kinsuji and hotsure.

The Senshuin school of Yamato had

moved to Akasaka in Mino during the
Muromachi period. The jigane and hamon
characteristics of this blade reflect the strong
Yamato influence in their work. The
vermilion-lacquered ribbed haft probably
dates from the Momoyama period. During
the Edo period vermilion mountings were
restricted to the use of families with a sound
military tradition.

31 Mounted naginata

Signed: Nantō jū Kanabō Hyoe no Jō Masatsugu
    ('Nantō [Southern Capital, Nara] resident in
    Kanabō [name of swordsmiths' group] Hyoe
    no Jō [title] Masatsugu [smith's name]')
Muromachi period, 16th century
L. (blade) 95.8 cm; (overall including mounting)
    189.0 cm

Naginata are thought to have been used in
battle since the Heian period. Their size
reflects the size of tachi of each period, and
generally in the Muromachi period they
were rather shorter than this piece, with a
broad head and very deep saki zori curve.
This naginata is long and of shallow curve,
rather like weapons of the Nambokuchō
period, and lacks the standard naginata
grooves. These weapons are also called
nagamaki, a term which strictly applies to
the mounting.

Like this smith, Masatsugu, members of
the Kanabo (or Kanefusa) group often used
ancient official military titles. They made
swords, naginata and yari of various shapes,
including the jumonji type with cross blades.
The group provided spears for the
celebrated spear-fighting monk Inei of the
Hōzōiin in Kōfukuji Temple during the early
Edo period, and one of their number
probably made the celebrated spear known
as Nippongo which belonged to the Kuroda
family. Like the Senshuin yari (no. 30), the
mounting is lacquered vermilion over black,
but with a helical wrapping under the
lacquer on the haft.

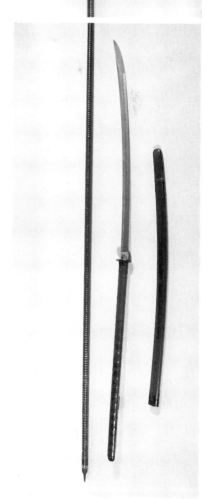

30 *left*, 31 *right*

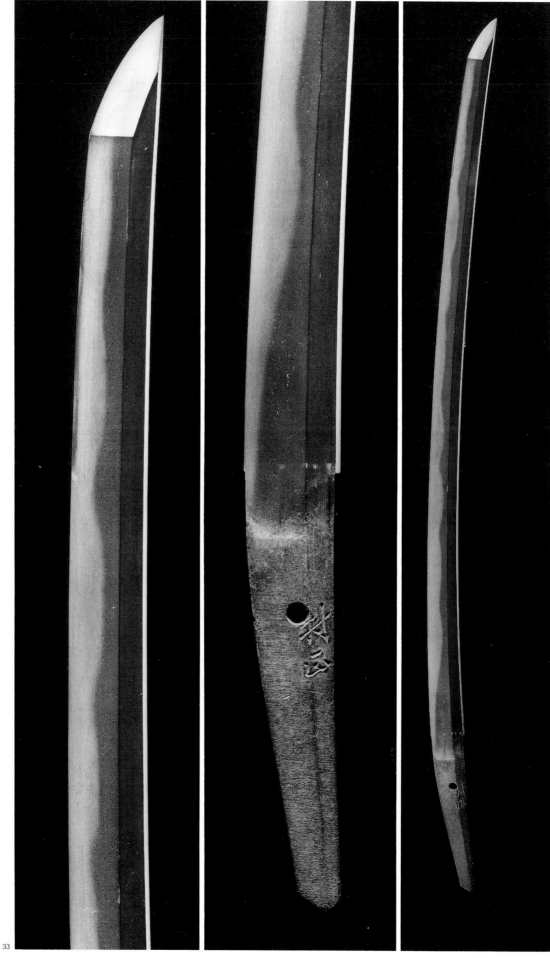

33

32 Yagyu Kanemoto *(illus. on p. 64)*

Muromachi period, 16th century
Signed: Kanemoto, Mino school
L. 62.3 cm

This uchigatana blade is of even breadth throughout its length, with a somewhat extended kissaki and pronounced saki zori curve. Uchigatana were worn through the belt with the edge uppermost, and as convention dictates that the signature should be on the side of the tang that faces outwards most swords from the middle Muromachi period onwards are signed, like this one, on the opposite side of the blade from tachi. The decrease in length reflects the change from mounted to foot combat. The saki zori curve was introduced for increased cutting efficiency, but it also facilitated drawing the sword.

The jigane is flowing itame, with jinie and the white shirake shadow common to Mino school work of this period. The hamon is small notare with a *yakidashi* (see p. 114), and variations of the sambon sugi pattern.

Kanemoto of Akasaka ranks together with Izumi no Kami Kanesada of Seki in skill. Their blades were highly regarded for their cutting ability. This blade is by Kanemoto II, who is generally known by the more familiar name Magoroku. He specialised in the sambon sugi hamon, which later generations contrived in a more regular form. The sword is named Yagyū Kanemoto since it was given by the swordsman Yagyū Munefūyū in 1665 to the Tokugawa Shogun together with a certificate of proficiency in kendō.

33 Katana blade *(illus. on p. 65)*

Muromachi period, 16th century
Signed: Muramasa (Muramasa II)
L. 75.8 cm
Sword Museum, Tokyo. Given by the late Prince Takamatsu

The shape of this sword is typical for an uchigatana of the late Muromachi period. The grain is flowing itame, and the hamon is notare, with intermingled gunome forming the same pattern along both sides of the blade, and sunagashi.

It seems there were three generations of smiths signing Muramasa. Their work is similar to that of Heianjō Nagayoshi and Kanesada of Seki, who worked in Mikawa and Yamada of Ise respectively, whose blades, like Muramasa's, are reputed to cut well. As Muramasa's work was considered unlucky for the Tokugawa family, the character *mura* was sometimes obliterated and the character *mune* inscribed beneath the remaining character thus transforming the signature into the far more palatable Masamune. It might have been this practice which gave rise to the popular belief that Muramasa was a pupil of Masamune of Sōshū, yet his earliest-known work is dated 1501, almost two centuries after Masamune's time.

34 Uchigatana blade

Dated: Bunmei Jūrokunen Hachigatsu Hi (a day in August 1474); Sue Bizen (late Bizen) school
Signed: Bizen Kuni Jū Osafune Katsumitsu Kojima nite saku ('Katsumitsu resident of Osafune village, Bizen Province, made at Kojima')
L. 65.5 cm

Many workshops produced large numbers of poor-quality blades during the late fifteenth and sixteenth centuries, but there were several excellent smiths like Yosozaemon no Jō Sukesada and the maker of this sword, Ukyō no Suke Katsumitsu, the father of Jirozaemon no Jō Katsumitsu (no. 35), who was succeeded by several generations of competent smiths.

This blade is typical of the shorter uchigatana suited to the infantry combat of the Sengoku period, made for single-handed use, and with a saki zori curve. The Sanskrit characters carved on the blade are religious in nature, but by this period had become very stylised and difficult to identify. The jigane is itame with jinie and lacks the vivid utsuri found on Bizen work before this time. The bright hamon with the typical varied gunome of the Sue Bizen school is predominantly in nie and contains the copious yō inevitably found on Sue Bizen work in both gunome and suguha.

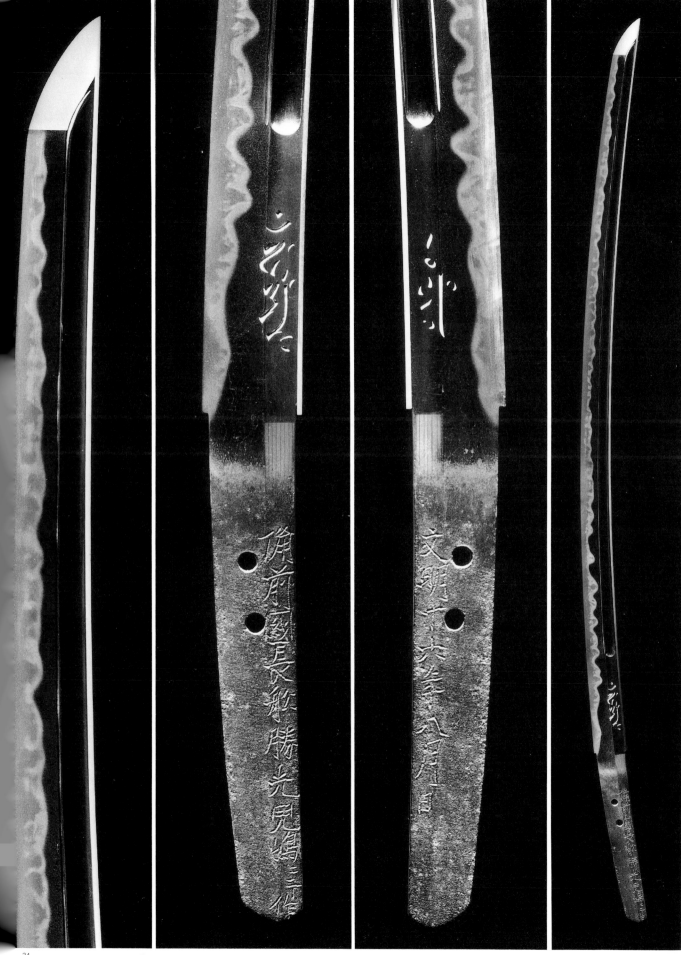

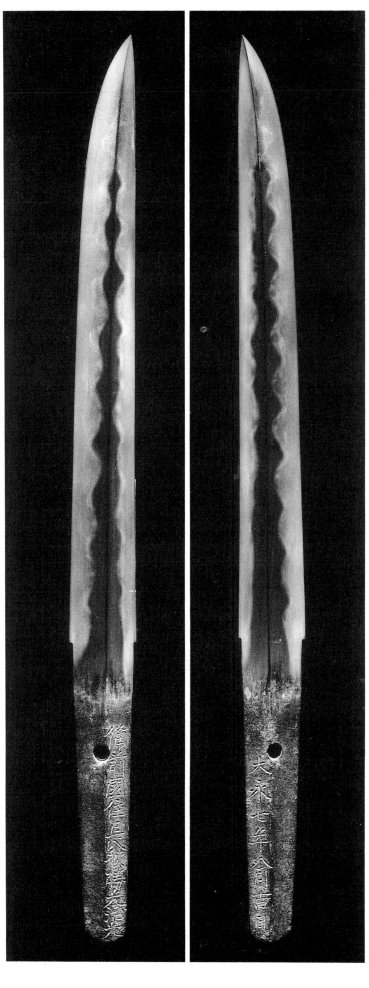

35 Tantō blade

Dated: Daiei Shichi Hachigatsu Kichijitsu (an
    auspicious day in August 1527)
Signed: Bizen Kuni Jū Osafune Katsumitsu
    Harumitsu ('Katsumitsu and Harumitsu resident
    in Osafune village, Bizen Province')
L. 21.3 cm
Sword Museum, Tokyo

Various different shaped tantō, like this
curved *moroha zukuri* ('double-edged')
weapon became popular from around the
beginning of the sixteenth century. At
around the same time the custom of making
hamon return deep down the back of even
some single-edged blades arose especially in
Bizen and Mino Provinces.

The itame jigane and lively gunome
hamon in nie which breaks at the high points
are representative of the work of the Sue
Bizen school. The blade was made jointly
by Katsumitsu and Harumitsu. Other joint
works exist by Jirozaemon no Jō Katsumitsu
together with Sakyō no Shin Munemitsu
and also Yosozaemon no Jō Sukesada.

36 Wakizashi blade

Muromachi period, 16th century
Signed: Hōki Kuni Kurayoshi Jū Sainoō Suke no
    Jō Hiroyoshi ('Sainoō [hereditary name] Suke
    no Jō [honorary title] Hiroyoshi [smith's name]
    resident at Kurayoshi in Hōki Province')
L. 45.4 cm

The blade has a square-ended bohi groove
on each side with a *soehi* accompanying
groove. The jigane is fine itame with
mokume, and the hamon is notare with
gunome and copious ashi, yō and some
sunagashi. There were at least twenty
smiths working in Hōki and signing
Hiroyoshi from the mid-fifteenth to the
seventeenth centuries, with some variations
in inscription. This sturdy blade belongs
with the mounting, no. 82, once possessed
by the swordsman Yagyū Munenori.

35

36

37 Tachi mounting

Muromachi period, 15th century
L. 122.7 cm
Kanagawa Prefectural Museum

An ito maki no tachi mounting with black
binding on both hilt and scabbard. The
scabbard is covered with leather, and with
all the fittings lacquered black, except for
the gilt paulownia mon menuki. The tsuba
is made of leather.

38 Uchigatana mounting

Muromachi period, 16th century
L. 106.3 cm
Tokyo National Museum

The scabbard is black-lacquered, or more properly *roiro*, or black which has turned slightly brown with the passage of time. The hilt is black-lacquered ray-fish skin wrapped with black-lacquered leather crossed over the end of the kashira in the style later demanded for formal wear during the Edo period. The only metal pieces on the mounting are the menuki, humble pieces of scrolling in openwork, and the fuchi, both of yamagane or unrefined copper. The kashira, kurikata and kaeri tsuno are of horn. The octagonal tsuba is of lacquered leather ply with two *ude nuki ana* through which a cord may be passed to secure the sword in the scabbard, and openings for a kōgai and a kozuka. Although leather tsuba were popular from the Kamakura to Muromachi periods on tachi mountings, this piece on an uchigatana mounting is exceptional. Indications of the age of the mounting include the large functional kurikata and kaeri tsuno, and the flattish section of the scabbard which slopes inwards in the direction of the cutting edge of the blade.

The mounting belonged with a sword which was given as a devotional offering to the Hōryūji Temple in Nara, and was kept for some centuries in the Saiendō Hall of that temple. It is known to date from around the Tenbun era (1532–54) from comparison with other material in the Saiendō collection. Very few uchigatana mountings survive from the Muromachi period, and this must therefore be considered a valuable study piece, expressing well the sombre standards of the pre-Momoyama period warrior class.

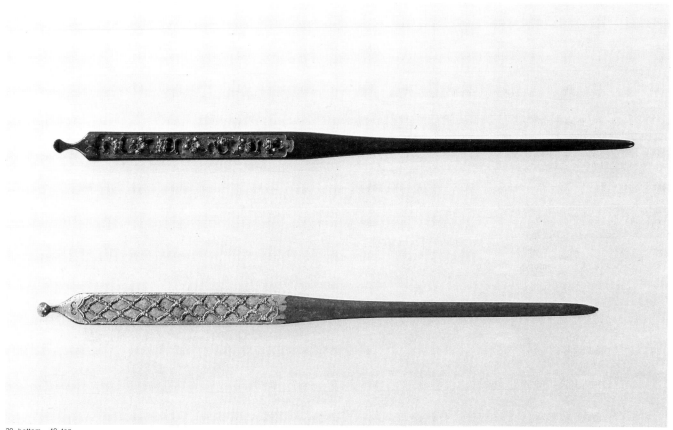

39 *bottom,* 40 *top*

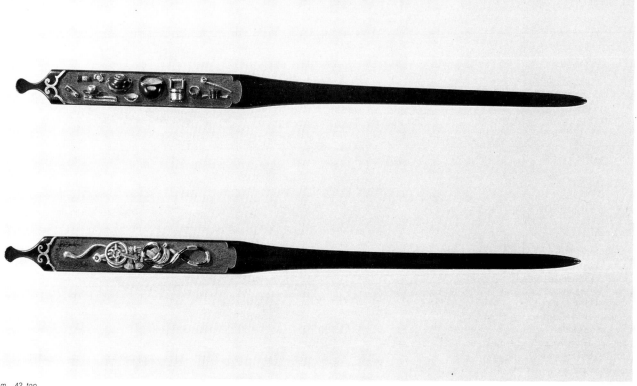

41 *bottom,* 42 *top*

39 Kōgai

Yamagane, decorated with gilded net pattern

Nambokuchō period, 14th century
L. 22.1 cm

40 Kōgai

Decorated with autumn grasses and details in gold-inlaid high-relief sculpture on shakudō nanako ground

Muromachi period, 16th century; early Mino school
L. 22.9 cm

41 Kōgai

Decorated with horse-trappings in gold-inlaid high-relief sculpture on shakudō nanako ground

Muromachi period, 16th century
Unsigned; attributed to Gotō Jōshin (1505 or 1512–62)
L. 22.9 cm

This rich shakudō piece is decorated with details in overlaid gold foil by the method known as *uttori* which is common to early Gotō work.

43   *enlarged × 2*

42 Kōgai

Decorated with Tea Ceremony utensils in gold-inlaid high-relief sculpture on shakudō nanako ground

Muromachi-Momoyama period, 16th century; early Gotō school
L. 22.6 m

As one of the arts supported by the Ashikaga Shoguns, who retained the Gotō family, the Way of Tea was a natural subject for sword-fittings.

43 Menuki

Decorated with youths and oxen in gold, silver and shakudō

Muromachi period, 16th century; early Gotō family work
L. 2.9 cm

43   *enlarged × 2*

Young cowherds mounted on their oxen, or sometimes grooms with their horses, have been a popular subject in Japanese art since the Muromachi period. They often wear conical straw hats and play the flute, and are usually of a cheerful countenance. The theme originated in China, where they appear as catalysts to the main plots of stories, usually possessing unspoken supernatural powers or understanding.

44

45 Tsuba

Iron, pierced in positive silhouette with five-storeyed tower and invocation 'Hachiman Dai Bosatsu'

Muromachi period, 16th century; armour maker's work
H. 10.7 cm

The characters 'Hachiman Dai Bosatsu' ('Hail to the great Bodhisattva Hachiman') indicate reverence to the Buddhist aspect of the Shintō deity Hachiman. The five-storeyed tower also has Buddhist connotations, being the shape of reliquaries, temple towers and graves, and represents the 'five elements' of ground, fire, wind, water and nothingness. A further gold inscription on the tower reads 'Namu Amida Butsu' ('Hail to Amida Buddha').

44 Tsuba

Yamagane, *mokkō*-shape, carved with autumn grasses in relief on nanako ground

Muromachi period, 16th century; early Mino school
H. 6.1 cm

This tsuba is of an early tachi tsuba shape, pierced with four heart-shaped 'boar's eye' motifs signifying courage, yet it was made for an uchigatana mounting since it has an opening for a kozuka.

The early Mino school were makers of metal fittings for tachi-type sword mountings working in Mino Province during the early Muromachi period, but it is probable that the style flourished also among the metalworkers of Kyoto. Their work was typically deeply carved in the method known as *sukidashi bori* ('carving by scooping out'), and the lowered ground was often decorated with nanako punch marks. Many pieces are decorated with gold-sheet overlay. Their themes were most often nature, with flowers, grasses and sometimes animals. The first master of the Gotō school, Yūjō, was schooled in the early Mino style.

46 Tsuba

Iron, pierced in negative silhouette with tower and sickle

Muromachi period, 16th century; armour maker's work
H. 10.1 cm

The Buddhist tower is found frequently on early armourers' work (no. 45). The tower often extends upwards by means of extra piercings which might have served as ude nuki ana (see no. 38). Examples of similar work depict raindrops as sets of two pierced holes, possibly also for that purpose. The sickles were used for rice harvesting and ground clearing, and in certain rural areas were attached to weighted chains to make weapons called *kusari gama*. Together the sickles and tower allude to the transient nature of human life.

45

46

47   enlarged by 30%

47 Tsuba

Iron, pierced in positive silhouette with
stylised plovers and waves

Muromachi period, 16th century; Owari school
H. 8.2 cm

Typically for the Owari school, the rim of
the tsuba is somewhat thicker than the
centre and slightly gnarled around the edge.
The iron is of a rich dark colour, with the
hammered surface texture known as *tekkotsu*
('iron bones') which results from the layered
structure of the forged metal.

48 Tsuba

Iron, pierced in positive silhouette with
raimon, or 'lightning pattern'

Muromachi period, 16th century; Owari school
H. 8.3 cm

49 Tsuba

Iron, with brass inlay of mon and leafy
tendrils

Muromachi period, 16th century; Heianjō school
H. 8.2 cm

Heianjō-type tsuba decorated with grasses
and family mon were made from around the
middle or late Muromachi period and into
the Edo period. The early work was iron
with brass inlay and usually pierced. The
style greatly influenced Edo period schools,
like those of Higo and the Shōami. Although
the name Heianjō implies a school in Kyoto,
it is probable that the style was widespread.

48   *enlarged by 30%*

49   *enlarged by 30%*

51

51 Helmet

Muromachi period, 16th century
H. (bowl) 14.3 cm
Kyoto National Museum

This suji kabuto is composed of forty-eight plates, lacquered black overall, and with the ridges all with gilt-copper rims. In akoda nari style, like no. 50, the helmet is remarkable for the richness of the gilt metalwork on the peak, with chrysanthemums sculpted on a nanako ground, and roundly carved shishi and peonies fixed over this by means of pins. Although the kuwagata are missing, the central crest in the form of an exotically shaped three-pronged vajra immediately draws the eye and adds to the dignity of the helmet. The high arrangement of the fukigaeshi and the shallow spread of the shikoro are further characteristics of the Muromachi period, resulting directly from the decreasing dependence on the bow in combat (p. 42).

50 Haramaki (illus. in colour on p. 83)

Muromachi period, 15th century
H. (cuirass) 28.0 cm; (helmet bowl) 14.0 cm
Important Cultural Property

The haramaki was developed as a result of the need for a lighter armour than the horseman's ōyoroi, which could weigh even as much as the wearer. The style became very popular during the Muromachi period both for low-grade warriors and their leaders, who in addition wore fine helmets. The haramaki springs around the body leaving a gap down the centre of the back. The kusazuri is composed of a greater number of looser linked rows of lacquered iron lamellae than the ōyoroi, enabling far greater freedom of movement.

This example is colourfully mounted with variegated braid and a suji kabuto. The ridges of the helmet plates are all rimmed with *fukurin* ('cladding rings') of bronze, the plates themselves being thickly lacquered over. The bowl of this helmet swells out at the back and slopes forward at the front in the style called *akoda nari*, after the *akoda* fruit (a kind of pumpkin), which was introduced in the Muromachi period. The fukigaeshi are somewhat smaller than those on earlier helmets which, together with the shikoro, are always arranged lower to protect the face and neck from the oblique front. They are decorated with gilt-copper roundels with chrysanthemums in relief, similar to the decoration on the other metal fittings. In place of kuwagata found on almost all helmets before the Muromachi period, this piece has a crest in the form of oak leaves.

52 Tōsei gusoku

Muromachi period, 16th century
H. (cuirass) 49 cm
Tower of London Armouries, XXV i2A

The cuirass, skirt and sode of this tōsei gusoku are composed of simple iron plates lacquered black. The severely functional helmet is a high-sided six-plate Etchū *nari* type. The kote are chain with the forearms well protected by iron plates.

Although of poor quality and simple construction, this armour is said to have belonged to a daimyō, Naito Yukiyasu. A Christian, he was exiled and is thought to have died in Manila in 1626. Worn gilt copper fittings on the armour bear his mon, a crucifix.

7

The Momoyama period
(1573–1600)

The Momoyama and early Edo period saw the emergence of new styles of swordmaking centred on the castle towns of the daimyō. Swords made after the first year of the Keichō era (1596) are considered by convention to be *shintō* ('new swords'), as opposed to *kotō* ('old swords') made before that date. A distinct fashion in sword shapes which had appeared in the Momoyama period persisted for a few decades into the historical Edo period. Demand for swords had naturally fallen in this era of peace. The great armies of commoners had been disbanded, and attempts made to disarm the general populace. Toyotomi Hideyoshi had instituted a *katana gari* ('sword hunt') in 1588, prohibiting farmers and such people from possessing swords, bows and arrows, spears and guns. The great centres of production, like Osafune in Bizen and Seki in Mino, could no longer support large numbers of smiths, and the most accomplished smiths naturally migrated to the provincial towns to find work under the patronage of the daimyō.

Since the most valued possession for the samurai was his sword, there was a great demand among the better off for fine blades of the Kamakura and Yoshino periods. The fashion was for wearing a daisho in uchigatana-type mountings, which necessitated cutting down the ancient long swords to a convenient length of around 70 cm. Due to this *suriage* practice many old swords lost their original tangs, and thus the inscriptions on them. A few Nambokuchō period tachi survive in their original length, or close to it, but most have been drastically shortened. The work of the Sōshū smiths, Yukimitsu, Masamune and the following generation are therefore usually not signed but bear inscriptions, sometimes inlaid in gold, by sword appraisers identifying their maker.

The early shintō smiths copied the fashionable shape of these cut-down weapons, which were naturally broad and thin, with an even shallow curve and long kissaki. They further emulated the old traditions, although the finer secrets of manufacture must have been lost by this time. Some of the schools which were established during this period continued for several generations under the patronage of the provincial daimyō, each producing swords in their distinctive style.

Several of the greater provincial smiths were schooled in the studio of one Umetada Myōju of Kyoto, who

claimed twenty-fifth generation ancestry from the Heian period master, Sanjō Munechika.

Umetada Myōju (d. 1631)
Myōju made mostly hira zukuri-type daggers in Shizu style, with fine, bright, flowing itame grain, and gentle, undulating or gunome hamon in nie. There is only one extant long sword which bears his signature (no. 53). He was a versatile metalworker and also made metal sword-fittings (p. 90). The *Umetada Oshigata shū* (1641), which contains records of Myōju's inscriptions on swords, contains evidence that, like the Honami family, he was commissioned to cut down old swords to a length suitable for the uchigatana type of mounting. Myōju was a skilful sculptor on sword blades as well as in soft metal fittings. Whereas carvings on the blades of swords had hitherto primarily expressed the religious beliefs of the samurai, Myōju used his blades as vehicles for decorative sculpture in the artistic spirit of the Momoyama period. His pupils included such eminent smiths as Horigawa Kunihiro (no. 54), Higo no Kami Teruhiro, Harima no Kami Teruhiro, Tadayoshi of Hizen (no. 55), Yamato Daijō Yoshinobu and Muneyoshi, or Munenaga, of Yamashiro. Myōju died in 1631 at the age of seventy-four.

Horigawa Kunihiro (d. 1614)
As a *rōnin*, or masterless samurai, Kunihiro roamed Japan studying his chosen career of swordsmith. His early work dates from the start of the Tenshō era (1573–91) when he lived in Furuya of Hyūga Province. From the early Keichō era (1596–1614) he lived in Ichigo Horikawa in Kyoto. Kunihiro nurtured many famous pupils up until his death at the age of eighty-four in 1614. His swords have a rather vivid jihada full of jinie and a rich hamon of large nie in notare, gunome and midare, and all the variations in structure found on the work of the early Sōshū masters. Indeed, one of his greatest works, the Yamauba Giri ('Mountain Hag Cutter') made around 1590, was a copy of a tachi made by Chōgi, one of the pupils of Masamune, commissioned by the master of Ashikaga Castle in Noshū Province, Nagao Akinaga.

The Sanpin smiths
These were the sons of Kanemichi of Seki, who has been

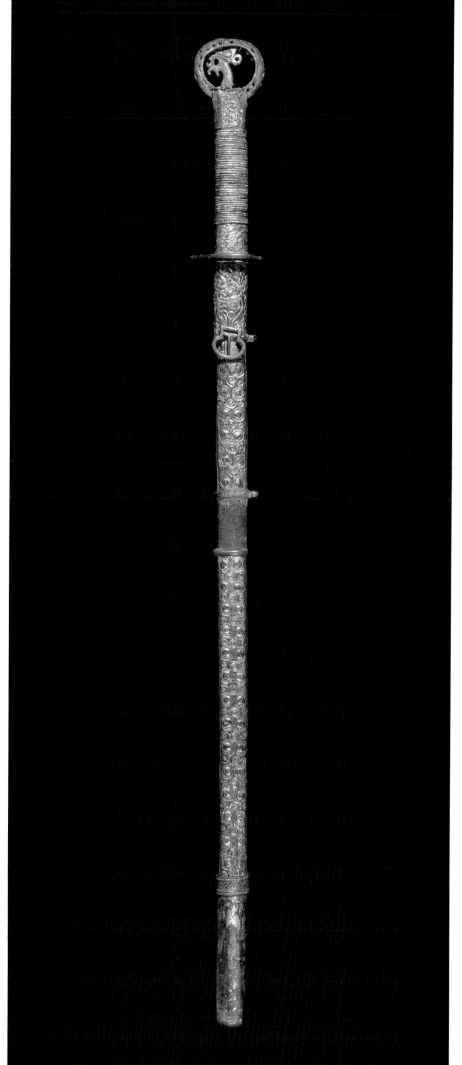

3   front

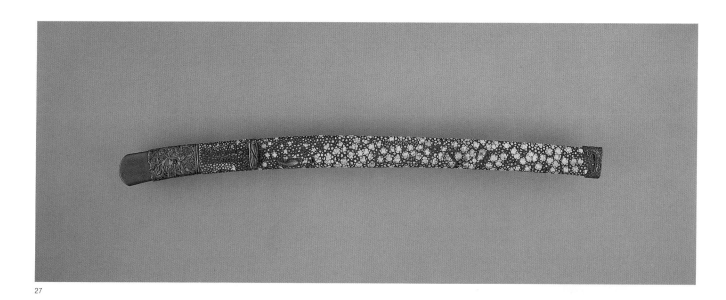

27

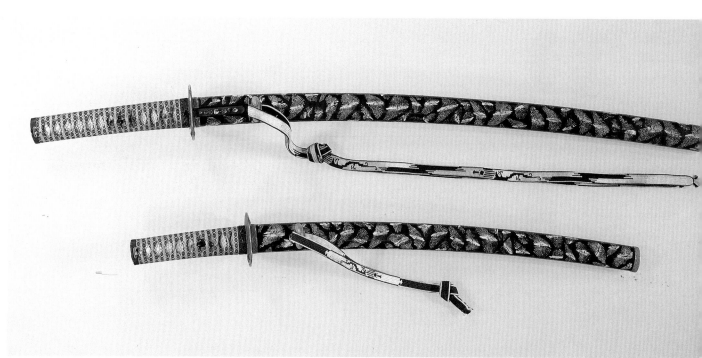

85

86

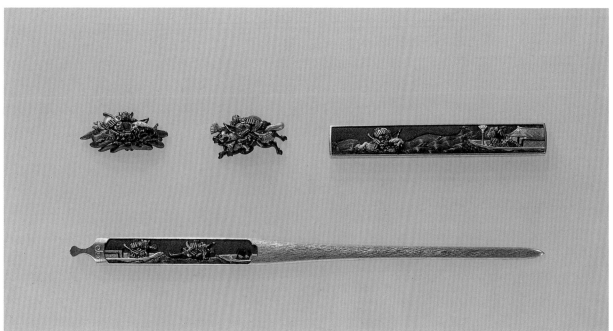

108 *enlarged by 30%*

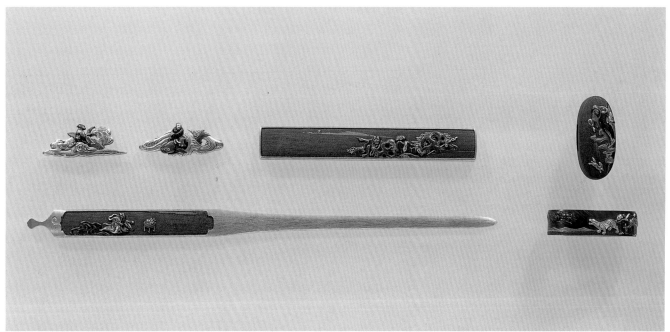

128 *enlarged by 30%*

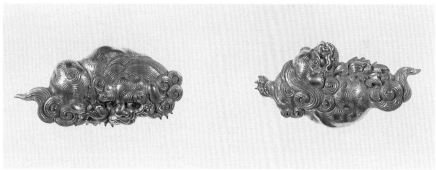

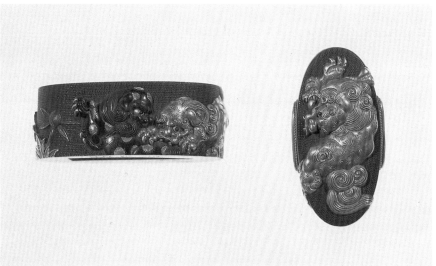

113   *enlarged by 30%*

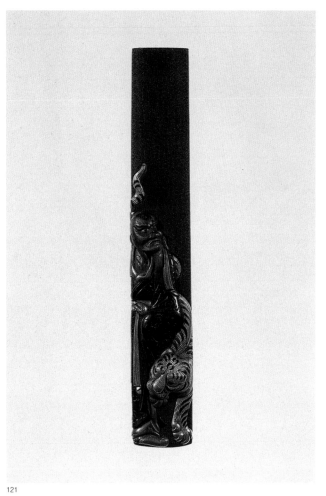

121

129   *enlarged by 30%*

described as the ninth generation after Shizu Saburō Kaneuji. Their swords are in Mino style, with notare, gunome midare or suguha in gentle nie. The jigane is a flowing itame or sometimes masame, with masame on the shinogi ji, a common feature on most shintō blades influenced by the Mino tradition.

The first generations, Iga no Kami Kinmichi, Rai Kinmichi, Tamba no Kami Yoshimichi and Etchū no Kami Masatoshi, made broad blades in Momoyama style based on the tradition of the Shizu school. In his later years Yoshimichi introduced decorative hamon, like *sudareba* (a kind of bamboo curtain). His son moved to Osaka, where he devised yet more exotic hamon patterns like *kikusui* ('chrysanthemums floating along a river').

Hashimoto Shinzaemon Tadayoshi of Hizen (1572–1632)

Tadayoshi was adopted into a swordsmith's studio on the death of his father, when he was only twelve or so years old. He went to Kyoto for three years between 1596 and 1598, studying under Umetada Myōju, from whose name he received the first character, *tada*, of Tadayoshi. Thereafter he was appointed as swordsmith to the ruling Nabeshima family of Hizen Province, and worked in the castle town of Saga. Tadayoshi's work reflected the style of his teacher, Myōju, with notare-style hamon of nie and clear itame hada. The name Tadayoshi continued for several generations, all of whom produced fine-quality work in a similar style. The characteristic Hizen hada is the finest koitame with even jinie, known as *konuka* ('rice flower') hada, which was used as a face powder by women. The hamon is often suguha, or gunome midare. In style modelled on work of the Rai school of the Kamakura period, the shapes of the blades are elegant and the curve deeper than that of most shintō swords. The Hizen smiths also made a large chōji hamon, with long ashi reaching straight down almost to the cutting edge. Their boshi is typically a delicate *komaru* ('small round type') on the best work.

Yasutsugu of Echizen

Yasutsugu originated in Shimosaka of Ōmi Province, and it is thought that he signed Shimosaka on some of his early work. He obtained the first character, *yasu*, of his name from Tokugawa Ieyasu, who employed him as the leader of the Shimosaka studio to make swords in Edo. Both Yasutsugu I and the second generation lived in Edo and Echizen alternately, but the family split into two groups from the third generation onwards. Yasutsugu's blades are often inscribed indicating that they were made with *namban tetsu* ('southern barbarian iron'), or imported iron. He was commissioned to make copies of famous heirloom swords, especially Sōshū-school blades. Ieyasu gave Yasutsugu the right to carve the triple hollyhock mon of the Tokigawa family on the tangs of his swords, which privilege his descendants kept.

Kashū Kanewaka

Kanewaka worked in the castle town of the Maeda clan, Kaga. His work was predominantly in Mino style, and he is famous for his large undulating hako notare hamon rich in nie. The school continued for several generations.

Nanki Shigekuni

Shigekuni is said to have originally worked in the Yamato Tegai tradition before moving to Ki Province. Some of his work reflects the old Yamato style with flowing or masame jigane and hamon which are basically suguha with nijuba, hotsure and uchi no ke, like Kamakura period Tegai blades. However, he also worked in the Sōshū style, modelling his blades on those of Gō Yoshihiro, the pupil of Masamune.

Noda Hankei

A gunsmith called Shigetaka in the employ of the Tokugawas left Edo upon the retirement of Ieyasu in 1607 and went to live in Suruga. For some years he made both swords and guns, until Ieyasu died in 1616, when he returned again to Edo. Hankei, as he now styled himself, made swords with steels of different quality, producing vivid ō ('large') itame grain, somewhat similar to that of Etchū Norishige in the fourteenth century, whose work he must have emulated. Hankei's hamon are broad and violent, full of activity with running lines of kinsuji and sunagashi. Tradition has it that his body was discovered cut in two in the streets of Edo, no doubt having fallen victim to the barbaric practice of *tsuji giri* (see p. 113) at the hand of an unknown assailant.

Some smiths still worked in the traditional centres: in Bungo there was the Takada school, in Chukugo Onizuka Yoshikuni, and in Osafune Hikobei no Jō Sukesada preserved the Bizen tradition, which was also carried on in Edo and elsewhere by branches of the Ishido school. Other smiths of the period included Hida no Kami Ujifusa and Sagami no Kami Masatsune, working in their own versions of the Mino style in Owari (Nagoya).

Sword-fittings

The castle towns bred traditions of sword-fittings makers as well as swordsmiths in the Momoyama and Edo periods. In Higo, for example, several makers flourished under the Hosokawa daimyō: there were Hayashi Matashichi who worked in iron, Hirata Hikozō who used copper and brass and enamelling, Shimizu Jingo, Nishigaki Kanjirō and others. Much of their work employed brass inlay on an iron ground, often with a pierced design.

Colourful mountings were fashionable. Gold or vermilion-lacquered scabbards required correspondingly luxurious metal fittings. In Kyoto the versatile artist Umetada Myōju (p. 80, no. 62), who also made swords, specialised in the level inlay of a number of different metals, including copper, shakudō and brass, on soft metal tsubas in addition to ironwork. Also in Kyoto the Kyō sukashi workers made tsuba after the style of the earlier Heianjō sukashi. A number of these tsuba makers from Kyoto settled at Akasaka in Edo where they produced work similar to the Kyoto style but with a wider and more lively repertoire of design. They are known to have influenced a branch of the Myōchin armourers in Tosa Province who had turned their hand to the manufacture of tsuba.

In Echizen the Akao, Kinai and Nagasone schools specialised in vigorous pictorial work roundly carved in yō sukashi. The Kinai had some connection with the Yasutsugu family of swordsmiths, and often carved dragons similar to those found on sword blades.

Horimono

Whereas previously horimono were essentially religious in nature, during the Momoyama period their purpose was to a great extent purely decorative, and even the deities depicted in a light-hearted fashion. Umetada

Myōju set new fashions, with his dragon ascending one side of the blade in pursuit of the hōkyū ('treasure jewel' of Buddhism), and a second dragon descending the other. Myōju's dragons are quite different from their predecessors. They are not so energetic as those of the Muromachi period, yet they are beautifully carved, with large lower jaws and humorous twinkling eyes. There were few kurikaras carved in this period, and the dragons signify popular mythology rather than the deep concepts of esoteric Buddhism. Dragons were also depicted with their tails in the form of ken, alluding to the creation legends recorded in the Kojiki ('Record of Ancient Matters', AD 712). The myth tells how the Shintō deity Susano O no Mikoto overwhelmed a dragon, the Yamata no Oroshi, and having broken his sword on the creature's tail was rewarded with another which magically emerged from the wound. The sword is called Kusanagi no Tsurugi and is identified with the Ame no Muro Kumo no Tsurugi of the Nihon Shōki (AD 720).

From now on the motifs are picturesque, and figures of deities presented in a more human aspect. Myōju's strong use of the chisel was inherited by the Horigawa pupils. Zen motifs are found from this period, like the patriarch Bodhidarma, and the pair of priests Kanzan and Jittoku. Specialist carvers worked for smiths in the provinces. In Hizen the swords of Tadayoshi were sculpted, often with dragons, by sculptors signing Yoshinaga or Munenaga. Their dragons are delicate and shallowly carved, centred on the shinogi of the blade, and have characteristic long slender necks. In contrast, dragons carved by the Kinai studios of Echizen on swords made by the Yasutsugu family are robust, with large scales deeply carved into the shinogi ji. Yasutsugu and his school copied work of the early Sōshū smiths, and pierced horimono are often evident on their swords.

Armour

Types of armour developed as a result of the advent of firearms and massed warfare by armies of foot soldiers culminated in the manufacture of the tōsei gusoku ('equipment of the times'). Designed to protect as much of the body as possible from missiles and cutting weapons, and yet remain light enough to afford sufficient mobility, the tōsei gusoku often consisted of a matching set of helmet, mask, cuirass, kote, sode, haidate and suneate. Some armour was made on European lines with solid iron cuirasses in order to withstand gunfire (no. 73), and these are sometimes found bearing bullet marks. This was an age when any man of prowess could rise through the ranks and achieve personal fame and power, and the many styles of tōsei gusoku reflect this emphasis on the individual. Some armours were made with exotic helmets in the form of animal heads, deities, sea beasts and so on, drawing attention to the wearer on the battlefield. Red, silver and gold lacquer were used to startling effect. *Jimbaori*, surcoats usually of leather of textile, were short-sleeved, and decorated strikingly with all kinds of motifs in addition to family mon.

53 Katana blade *(illus. on p. 92)*

Dated: Keichō sannen Hachigatsu Hi (a day in August 1598)
Signed: Yamashiro Kuni Nishijin Jū Nin Umetada Myōju ('Umetada Myōju, a man resident in Nishiji, Yamashiro [Kyoto]') and Ta E Kore Watasu Bekarazu ('Do not give this to another')
L. 64.7 cm
Kyoto National Museum, Important Cultural Property

The blade is broad with an extended kissaki and a shallow even curve in the style of cut-down long blades of the Nambokuchō period. The jigane is a serene itame with flowing patches and fine jinie. The hamon is notare in small nie.

Beneath a bohi on one side of the blade is an inset panel with a Sanskrit character and Fudō Myō-Ō, whilst the other side has an ascending dragon with a tail in the form of a ken-type sword. Both exemplify Myōju's masterly hand at decorative carving, which was passed on to several pupils (p. 80). The date on this sword, 1598, is the earliest-known inscribed on a work by Umetada Myōju (1158–1618, p. 80), the master metalworker of Kyoto active during the Momoyama period. The sword is also the only known long sword made by him, although many tantō survive. The signature is on the side traditionally used for tachi, like the customary signatures of his pupil, Tadayoshi of Hizen (p. 89, no. 55), and the Hizen school. Judging from the inscription on the tang, Myōju valued this sword highly and probably gave it to a dear friend.

54 Katana blade *(illus. on p. 93)*

Momoyama period, *c.* 1610
Signed: Fujiwara Kunihiro (d. 1614 aged 84)
L. 67.5 cm
Important Art Object

Swords of the Momoyama period were modelled on the shapes of the cut-down swords of the Kamakura and Nambokuchō periods, and many, like this example and the katana by Tadayoshi of Hizen (no. 55), are of correspondingly shallow curve and even width. The jigane of this blade is a vivid flowing itame, covered with jinie and splashes of chikei. The hamon swells out at the yakidashi, continues as a broad suguha with gunome and small midare, and broadens in large midare at the monouchi. There is much hotsure and sunagashi throughout.

The sword is one of Kunihiro's later works, a so-called Keichō uchi, made in the Keichō era (1596–1614), or Horikawa uchi, named after his later residence in Horikawa, Kyoto. During this period he made fine blades in Shizu style like this example, although he also emulated other Sōshū tradition smiths and the suguha style of the Kamakura period Rai school.

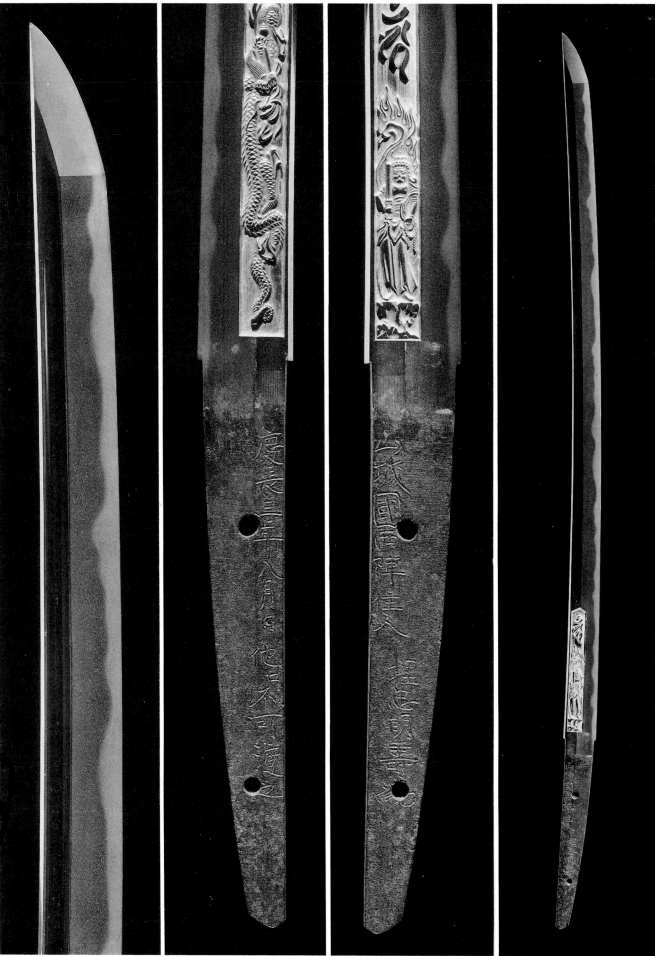

55 Katana blade

Momoyama period, *c.* 1610
Signed: Hizen Kuni Tadayoshi. Tadayoshi I of
   Hizen Province (1572–1633)
L. 69.0 cm

The even breadth of this blade and its
elegant shallow curve with a slightly
elongated kissaki identify it as a Momoyama
period work of the finest quality.

The jigane is koitame rich in jinie and
chikei. The hamon is notare with gunome,
with delicate sunagashi in places in the style
of the fourteenth-century Shizu school.
Tadayoshi also worked in a fine suguha
hamon, in the style of the Enju school of
Higo. Like all fine work by the early
generations of Tadayoshi's family, the boshi
has the finest komaru, slightly hakikake, or
swept along.

The horimono are a kurikara with *tsume*
('claws'), and a vajra-hilted ken-type sword.
The work is by the specialist carver
Munenaga, whose dragons are
characteristically short and centred on the
shinogi.

Tadayoshi I studied under Umetada
Myōju (p. 80, no. 53) in Kyoto between
1596 and 1598, and returned again for a
further period some time in the Genna era
(1615–24). In the tenth year of Genna he
received the title Musashi Daijō and
changed his name to Tadahiro. His son Ōmi
Daijō Tadahiro, the third-generation Mutsu
no Kami Tadayoshi, and their descendants
throughout the Edo period, continued in the
service of the Nabeshima clan in Saga. Their
jigane developed into the finest of small
itame with delicate evenly spread jinie which
is popularly known as *konuka hada* ('rice
flour skin'), named after rice powder which
ladies used as a cosmetic. The hamon of
most Hizen swords are bright suguha in nie,
but there is also large gunome, and large
round-headed chōji with deep ashi reaching
sometimes down to the cutting edge.

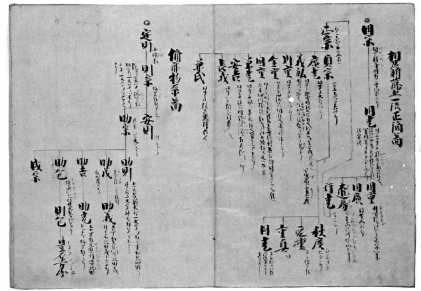

56

56 Takeya Hiden Shō ('Takeya Secret Document')

Ink on paper
1605
Takeya Sōzaemon Nyūdō Sōmai
24.5 × 19.0 cm
Sword Museum, Tokyo

This record of swordsmiths compiled by the
sword polisher Takeya Sōmai of Owari
Province contains a wealth of information
on the early schools. The pages illustrated
contain on the right a version of the Sōshū
lineage starting with Bizen Saburō
Kunimune, next Shintōgo Kunimitsu,
followed by Yukimitsu and then Masamune
with his ten pupils, and four pupils of
Sadamune. On the left is a lineage of the
Bizen school.

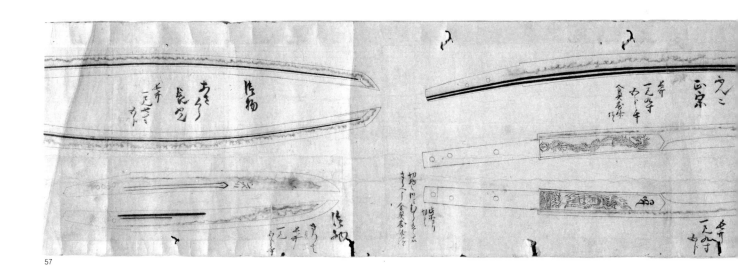

57

58

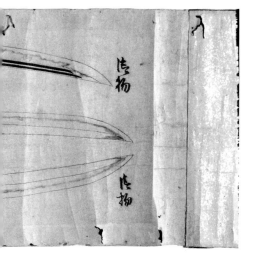

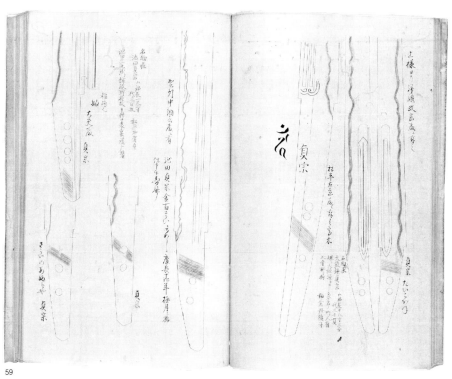

59

57 Record of swords

Handscroll, ink on paper
1615
Copy by Umetada Jusai of original by Honami
  Kōtoku
21.1 × 34.0 cm
Tokyo National Museum, Important Art Object

The document contains drawings of a total
of seventy-three blades and records the
names of the swordsmiths, the lengths of
the blades and whether they were shortened
by Honami. Umetada Jusai added a further
eighteen swords and made note of those
swords which had been damaged in the fire
of Osaka Castle in the same year and those
for which the Umetada family had made
fittings.

The famous blades illustrated here are by
Masamune (top right), Yoshimitsu (bottom
right), Nagamitsu (top left) and Sadamune
(bottom left).

58 Kokin Meizukushi

Woodblock-printed book in seven volumes
1661
27.0 × 19.5 cm
Sword Museum, Tokyo

The *Kokin Meizukushi* ('List of Signatures
Past and Present') is the first printed book
on the subject of sword appraisal. It follows
the system of earlier documents of
recording names of smiths, their schools and
details of their work. It owes much to the
Muromachi period *Shinkan Hiden Shō* ('New
Edition Secret Document') and the work of
the Takeya family of sword polishers of
Owari Province. Although the book was
first published in 1661, an inscription in it
suggests an original date of 1611.

59 Umetada Oshigata Shū

Ink on paper
Edo period, 17th century
30.5 × 21.0 cm
Sword Museum, Tokyo

The book is a record of swords worked on
by the family of Umetada Myōju (p. 80).
This illustration shows swords by Sadamune
of Sōshū (p. 52, no. 25).

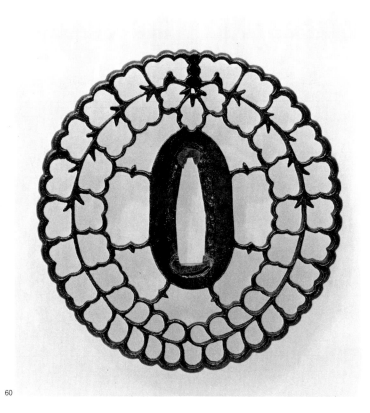

60

61

60 Tsuba

Iron, pierced with stylised trailing
wisteria and paulownia mon

Momoyama period, 16th century; Kyō sukashi
school
H. 8.6 cm

The wisteria was also used as a clan mon
design, so this tsuba could well represent
the joining of two families. Like most Kyō
sukashi work, it is both elegant in concept
and delicate in construction, in keeping with
the aristocratic air of Kyoto.

61 Tsuba

Iron, pierced in positive silhouette with
four *tomoe* mon

Momoyama period, 16th century; Kyo sukashi
school
H. 8.2 cm

The *tomoe*, or linked-commas motif, was
used as a mon by many samurai and
aristocratic families. The double-tomoe form
can be interpreted as a representation of yin
and yang, while the triple-tome motif is
often associated with Shintō deities,
especially Hachiman. It was frequently used
to decorate the ends of drums for both
shrine ritual and military use.

62 Tsuba

Decorated with oak bough with leaves
and acorns in level inlaid shakudō on
patinated *shinchū* (a form of brass)
ground

Momoyama period, 17th century
Signed: Umetada Myōju (1538–1631)
H. 8.1 cm

Umetada Myōju of Kyoto, who styled
himself the twentieth-generation descendant
of the swordsmith Sanjō Munechika, was
probably the most diverse metalworker in
Japanese history. As a maker of tsuba, he
was equally at home with iron and soft
metals. His designs were, like this tsuba, in
the energetic decorative style of
Momoyama period painting, ceramics and
lacquerware. As a swordsmith he is famed
as the teacher of several of the greatest
makers of the time, and was an adroit
sculptor of dragons and other popular motifs
on his daggers (see p. 90 and no. 53).

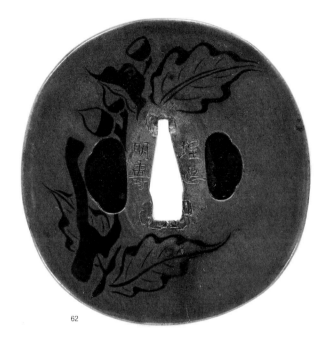

62

63 Tsuba

Iron, carved in sukidashi bori with bow and arrow of Hachiman

Momoyama period, 16th century
Signed: Nobuie
H. 8.1 cm

This tsuba is decorated in relief on the front with a bow and arrow, and on the reverse engraved with the invocation 'Namu Hachiman Dai Bosatsu' ('Hail to the great Bodhisattva Hachiman'). Hachiman is one of the deities who have a dual Buddhist and Shintō nature and is recognised in Shintō as the God of Archers. The same invocation is also often found carved on sword blades of the Muromachi period. The rich colour of the iron and simple elegance of the design compares with no. 64, also by Nobuie. The rims have been hammered to overlap the ground slightly.

63 *front*   63 *reverse*

64

64 Tsuba

Iron, mokko-shape, engraved with pine needles

Momoyama period, 16th century
Signed: Nobuie
H. 8.7 cm

The design of pine needles is often taken to represent marital fidelity, since they fall joined together in two.

Nobuie of Owari Province made rather thick iron tsuba with high relief, sometimes partially pierced, and engraved decorations. His designs, though often realistic, are evocative of the austerity of the life of the samurai at the end of the civil wars of the Sengoku period.

65 Tsuba *(illus. in colour on p. 105)*

Iron, carved in sukidashi bori with skull and bamboo shoots

Momoyama period, 16th century
Signed: Jōshū Fushimi jū Kaneie ('Kaneie resident of Fushimi in Jōshū Province')
H. 8.3 cm

As a *memento mori*, the skull is usually depicted together with something else, like wild grass, or in this case bamboo shoots, to express the desolation of an old battlefield. Bamboo, being resilient and long-lived, is itself a symbol of the samurai spirit, and it here emphasises the samurai's acknowledgement of the transitory nature of human life against the broader backcloth of his spiritual awareness. The rim of the tsuba has been characteristically hammered higher than the ground. One of the

68

66

67

openings for a kōgai has been plugged with gold-clad metal.

Kaneie is often considered to be the founder of the tradition of pictorial work on tsuba. He used thin iron plate, carving the ground away so that the designs appear in high relief, like the work of Nobuie of Owari (nos 63, 64), but also used gold and other metal inlay to depict details.

66 Kozuka
Decorated with mandarin ducks among lotuses in enamels on polished shakudō ground

Momoyama–Edo period, 17th century
Unsigned work of Hirata Dōnin (d. 1646)
L. 10.0 cm

Hirata Dōnin adapted the Chinese technology of cloisonné enamelling to Japanese taste for the decoration of sword-fittings. He was summoned to Edo to work for the government in 1611, where his descendants continued the work until this century. Hirata enamelling is done on either an iron or shakudō ground and employs gold wires for the cloisons.

67 Kozuka
Decorated with Mount Fuji in enamels and gold inlay on polished shakudō ground

Momoyama–Edo period, 17th century
Unsigned; attributed to Hirata Dōnin
L. 10.4 cm

This kozuka is decorated with the finest of coloured enamels typical of the early Hirata school. The subject of Mount Fuji must have been dear to the hearts of the people of Edo, since it was in those days clearly visible throughout most of the year. The mountain was also regarded as a deity in its own right, so this kozuka possibly had religious significance for the owner.

68 Uchigatana mounting
Edo period, 17th century
L. 103.8 cm
Tokyo National Museum

This mounting is in regulation kamishimo style (p. 113). The scabbard and ray-fish skin of the hilt are lacquered black, as is the horn kashira. The menuki are in the form of gold peonies. The fuchi is silver and the tsuba iron, both with level-inlaid shinchū mon. The kozuka and kōgai both have paulownia mon in high relief on a shakudō nanako ground. The silver *habaki* (retainer) has an inlaid chrysanthemum mon. It is a rare example of a tachi habaki whose profile follows the grooves in the blade, and the mouth of the scabbard retains the same profile.

The kiku gō saku tachi (no. 16) was formerly in the possession of the Uesugi family of Okushū Province, and is said to have been the favourite blade of a collection of thirty-five owned by Uesugi Kagekatsu. The present uchigatana-type mounting for the tachi blade was commissioned by Kagekatsu during the Genna era (1615–23).

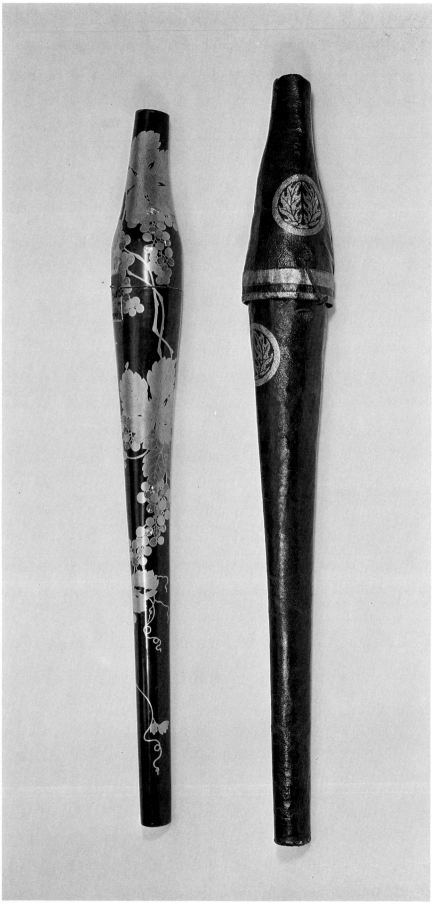

69 Sword travelling-case

Decorated with grapevine in gold makie and shell inlay on black ground

Momoyama period, late 16th or early 17th century
L. 112.5 cm
British Museum, JA 1902, 193

The gorgeous design of this piece is in grand Momoyama period style and was presumably part of a whole set of travelling equipment for a daimyō or other high-ranking samurai. Since the daimyō would spend much of his time travelling in a palanquin, his long sword would be carried by an attendant in such a case. The outer case is of leather, bearing a gilt oak-leaf mon.

70 Jimbaori

Feathers on hemp
Momoyama period, 16th century
L. 72 cm
British Museum, JA 1897, 3–18, 6. Given by Sir A. W. Franks

The decoration is formed from the feathers of two species of Japanese pheasant and a drake of an unidentified species of the genus *Anas* glued on to hemp. The collar is Chinese silk twill stiffened with paper. Originally simple serviceable coats to be worn over armour to keep out the elements, during the late Muromachi period the jimbaori, like armour itself, became an object of ostentation revealing the personal tastes of the wearer. They were decorated with motifs other than clan mon, like the target on this example.

71 Tōsei gusoku *(illus. in colour on p. 85)*

Momoyama period, 16th century
H. (cuirass) 49.0 cm
Agency for Cultural Affairs, Tokyo, Important Cultural Property

The cuirass is made of horizontal bands of black-lacquered iron forming the back and front which are hinged together on the left side. The kusazuri is composed of seven hanging sets of five linked lacquered plates. A dragon among waves of vermilion and silver lacquer decorates the lower parts of both cuirass and kusazuri. The haidate consists of two immense hanging pieces of chain-mail with chrysanthemum-shaped iron pieces at the knees. The suneate are each made of three hinged black-lacquered iron sheets, and extend up to form solid

knee protection. The sleeves are chain
overall, with sets of three hinged russet iron
plates over the forearms.

The helmet is of the suji kabuto type,
with a deep shikoro, and small fukigaeshi
bearing the 'Genji wheel' mon, which also
occurs on the cuirass, and on the gyōyō
flaps which hang over the shoulders. The
mask is russet iron, with a black moustache
and silver-lacquered teeth. The gilt crest on
the helmet is in the form of the vajra-hilted
ken-type sword blade of esoteric Buddhism.
This shape is that usually depicted in the
motif of the dragon with a sword in its tail,
and also in the kurikara motif of a dragon
coiled around a sword. The crest therefore
complements the dragon depicted on the
cuirass and the waves on the kusazuri. The
armour, which is depicted in the portrait
(no. 72), was owned by the daimyō of
Kozuke Province, Sakakibara Yasumasa
(1548–1606).

72 Portrait of Sakakibara Yasumasa (1548–1606)

(illus. in colour on p. 84)

Hanging scroll, ink and colours on paper
Momoyama period, 17th century
112.0 × 46.0 cm
Agency for Cultural Affairs, Tokyo, Important
 Cultural Property

The daimyō of Kozuke Province is shown
wearing the armour he was given by
Tokugawa Ieyasu (see no. 71). The pair of
sode are no longer with the armour.
Yasumasa is sitting on a bearskin rug armed
with a tachi and a wakizashi. In his gloved
right hand he carries a *saihai*, or signalling
baton. The *sashimono*, a flap which is fixed
on to a bracket on the back of the armour,
carries the sun and the stylised character of
mu, meaning 'nothingness'.

70

73 Tōsei gusoku

Momoyama period, 16th century
H. (cuirass) 45.0 cm
Agency for Cultural Affairs, Tokyo, Important
    Cultural Property

The high-breasted cuirass, in namban style,
is formed of two large beaten-out iron
sheets, the front and back linked by a hinge
on the left side. The outside of the cuirass
is patinated a gentle russet, and the inner
surfaces are clad with black-lacquered
leather which is visible at the raised edges
at the neck and arms. The sleeves are of the
Odagote type, with gourd-shaped iron
pieces for the upper and forearms mounted
over chain-mail. The kusazuri is composed
of five hanging sets of linked plates around
the front, and four at the back, joined with
blue braid. A large haidate formed of
lacquered leather plates hangs beneath the
kusazuri. The suneate are each composed of
six vertical iron strips linked by mail.

    The helmet is composed of two halves
joined vertically along the centre. A shroud
of white yak hair hangs over and around the
shikoro, at the ends of which two flaps bear
the 'Genji wheel' mon in gold lacquer. A
huge plume of yak hair is fitted on the back
of the helmet.

    Namban-style armour with components
based on non-Japanese originals became
popular during the second half of the
sixteenth century following the
introduction of firearms to Japan, since the
heavy iron plate gave far more protection
against gunfire than the traditional structure
of linked plates. The armour was given to
the daimyō of Kozuke Province, Sakakibara
Yasumasa (1548–1606), by Tokugawa
Ieyasu.

65   *enlarged × 2*

93   *enlarged × 2*

123 *enlarged × 2*

108

116   *enlarged × 2*

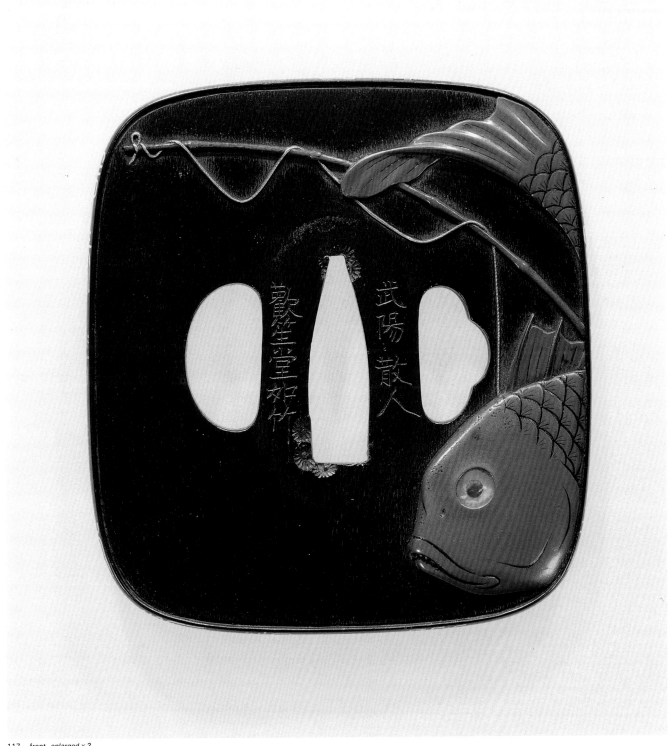

117 front, *enlarged × 2*

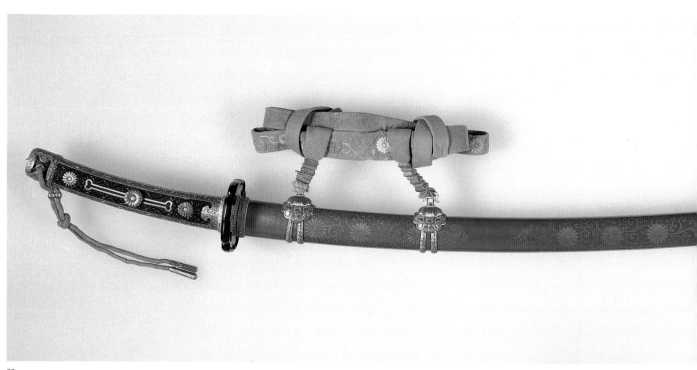

90

119

124

133   front, *enlarged by 30%*

134   *enlarged by 30%*

8

The Edo period

(1600–1868)

The first few decades of the Edo period saw the rapid expansion of the castle towns. Osaka and Edo especially rose from being little more than villages to rank among the world's largest cities by the middle of the seventeenth century. The Tokugawa government ruled strictly, preventing possible insurrection by imposing a number of regulations on the samurai class. For example, the Sankin Kotai system was introduced, whereby each provincial daimyō had to spend six months of the year living in Edo and leave his close family there when he returned for six months to his own lands. The family were therefore virtually hostages of the Tokugawas. Border guards were instructed to prevent the exit of women and the entry of guns into the capital. The activities of the provincial samurai were policed by a system of secret observers.

Each daimyō was allowed a castle with only a limited garrison, which rendered great numbers of the samurai jobless. These later became rōnin ('wave men'), with little means of livelihood. Some took respectable jobs as tutors of literature and calligraphy, others more menial jobs. Some abandoned their swords in an effort to fit into society, others devoted their lives to kendō practice, the best setting up dōjō ('place of the Way') behind closed doors. Many became vagabonds, or banded together in brotherhoods of lost causes. Among these brotherhoods the so-called kabukimono (from the verb kabuku, meaning 'to sway or swagger') caused the Tokugawas some alarm. Dressed in the showy styles of the Momoyama period, sporting extravagant hairstyles and long swords, they generally behaved in a boisterous manner.

Some rōnin had scant regard for life itself, and duels to the death were commonplace. The awful practice of tsuji giri (literally 'cutting at the crossroads') abounded. A rōnin eager to test his sword, or his skill, would lie in wait around the corner of a road junction for an innocent passer-by to appear and cut him down, escaping along the most open route. Swordsmen would roam the country testing their skill against all comers, hoping to prove their superiority to the masters of established fencing schools. One such rōnin, Miyamoto Musashi (1584–1645), invincible in combat, spent a lifetime searching for the deeper meaning in swordplay. He became enlightened at the age of fifty and spent the remainder of his life as a master of all arts and crafts. His ink paintings, in particular, are today among the highest regarded Zen-inspired art (no. 105).

The government took drastic measures to combat the menace of rōnin, and various edicts were passed, aimed at wiping them out. In 1645 unusual fashions in dress were banned, and the standard chomage hairstyle, with the front of the head shaven and the hair drawn up in a queue, was decreed for samurai. The employment of rōnin was prohibited, and the kabukimono brotherhood was banned. The wearing of swords over 2 shaku and 8 or 9 sun in length (about 80 cm) was prohibited, as were vermilion scabbards, which had been fashionable in the Momoyama period. The use of large square tsuba, which could be used as a step to climb over walls and barriers, was forbidden.

Samurai in service had to wear a standard dress of haori (jacket), and hakama (pleated divided trousers), known as a kamishimo ('top and bottom'), of subdued colour. Their clan mon had to be displayed on their clothes. Particularly when officially in residence in Edo, they had to wear a daisho, or 'matching pair of swords', in accordance with a published convention.

A number of further edicts were published during the seventeenth century limiting the possession of arms. The Shogun Tsunatoshi ruled in 1683 that musicians and painters should not carry long swords, even if they were of the samurai class, and that commoners could carry a dagger. Other edicts limited the carrying of swords by certain classes of people, including doctors and priests, to a short sword permitted on journeys between towns.

Perhaps as a result of the above regulations, as well as the style of kendō using large circular downward cuts which had evolved in the dōjō traditions, and convenience in carrying, the shape of the sword changed significantly around the middle of the seventeenth century. Becoming straighter and narrowing rather towards the kissaki, swords of this shape are sometimes called Kambun shintō (nos 75, 76), after the Kambun era (1661–73). The new shape became adopted in Edo, Osaka and some of the provinces. However, some schools, like that of Tadayoshi of Hizen, continued to make deeply curved swords according to the old tradition.

The styles of blades in Osaka in the west and Edo in the east differed. Whereas in the Momoyama and early

Edo periods the major smiths strove to emulate the work of the old kotō traditions, and continued to do so in many of the provincial castle towns, Edo and Osaka were large free markets where each smith needed to establish his own unique style in order to draw clientele.

The population of Edo at any time was composed largely of samurai, with the huge mansions of the provincial daimyō being occupied by sizeable retinues for half the year in accordance with the Sankin Kotai system. Osaka, on the other hand, was the centre for commerce and industry, and the population was largely of the merchant class. Furthermore, Osaka was near to Kyoto, and must have been influenced by its courtly fashions. The style in swords was correspondingly different. Generally the Osaka smiths contrived grandiose and eye-catching hamon patterns, while the Edo smiths' work was rather more subdued.

Osaka

The blades of Osaka have a finely forged hada and are of elegant proportions. Their flamboyant hamon slope down towards the *hamachi* (the end of the cutting edge separating the blade from the tang) in a sweeping line, or *yakidashi*, likened to the slopes of Mount Fuji.

Prominent Osaka smiths were descended from the Kyoto schools, and in particular from the school of Horikawa Kunihiro. Kawachi no Kami Kunisuke had been schooled by Kunihiro, and then by Kunitomo of the Horikawa school, before moving to Osaka. His son, known as Naka Kawachi, developed a distinctive *kobushi gata* ('fist-shaped') chōji. He had several pupils who made similar work, including Soboro Sukehiro from Harima Province. Sukehiro I's pupil, Tsuda Echizen no Kami Sukehiro, initially made chōji midare hamon like his teacher but later developed the so-called *tōran* hamon, resembling great sea waves, on blades having the finest of bright koitame grain. Many Osaka smiths copied this hamon, notably Sukehiro II's adopted son Ōmi no Kami Sukenao (no. 75).

Another smith from Harima, Ōmi no Kami Tadatsuna, also went to Osaka, producing large chōji midare with the fine grain typical of Osaka work. His pupil, known as Ikkanshi Tadatsuna, made swords with Sukehiro's tōran ha pattern and skilful carved decorations on his blades, especially dragons.

Izumi no Kami Kunisada, also from the school of Kunihiro, made swords with the typical Osaka-style fine grain and large gunome midare hamon. His pupil, Kunisada II, emulated Gō Yoshihiro (see p. 52), with broad hamon of nie in suguha or ō notare midare. Towards the end of the Kambun era he took Buddhist orders and adopted the name Shinkai (meaning 'True Renewal'). Numbered among the very best makers of his age, he surpassed his teacher's work and was given the right to carve the mark of the Imperial chrysanthemum on the tangs of his swords.

Edo

A notable school which continued for several generations in Edo was the Ishidō group, who made blades with complex chōji hamon in Bizen style, somewhat different from the rounded midare chōji of the Osaka Ishidō smiths like Kunisuke and Sukehiro. Other branches of the school were active in Kii and Chikuzen Provinces.

Yasutsugu's descendants continued to work for the Tokugawa government in Edo. Other Echizen smiths came to Edo, like Yamato no Kami Yasusada, whose blades were renowned for their extreme sharpness. In addition, Kazusa no Suke Kaneshige, Hojōji Masahiro and their pupils also made dignified blades with modest suguha or notareba hamon. However, the greatest of the smiths of Edo during this period, and probably the one whose name is today the most revered of all shintō smiths, was Nagasone Kotetsu (c. 1605–78, no. 76). Kotetsu was an armour maker from Nagasone village in Ōmi Province who worked for many years in Fukui of Echizen. He went to Edo to settle in Shimodani when he was fifty-one, there adopting the name Kotetsu, first using the characters for 'old iron', and then the characters reading 'tiger piercing'. He worked in suguha, ko notare with gunome in Mino style, and later made many swords in pure forms of gunome. He devised a particular form of regular gunome which has come to be called *juzuba*, or 'rosary hamon', since it resembles a row of rosary beads. In his early period Kotetsu made swords in the Nambokuchō shape, sometimes of katakiri ha type, and a large number of wakizashi. He was a skilful carver, and many of his swords bear figures of deities and Sanskrit invocations. Like the swords of Kaneshige and Yasusada, those of Kotetsu had a reputation for cutting efficiency. Many of his early works are inscribed in gold on the tangs with the results of cutting tests signed Yamano Kauemon or Kanjūrō.

The Genroku era (1688–1704)

Swordmaking declined in the last decades of the seventeenth century, no doubt due to the lack of demand for swords in peaceful times. Apart from the work of Ikkanshi Tadatsuna in Osaka, few swords were made in the last decades of the seventeenth and first decades of the eighteenth centuries. However, during this time the studios of decorative sword-fittings makers prospered, indicating perhaps the extent to which the sword as a fashionable accessory had replaced the sword as a weapon.

An interest in the martial arts, and particularly in swordmaking, was revived largely through the efforts of the eighth Tokugawa Shogun, Yoshimune (1684–1751), who was appointed to office in 1716. He summoned two smiths of Satsuma Province to Edo, Ichi no Hira Yasuyo and Miyahara Masakiyo; for the smiths of Satsuma and other provinces removed from the capital had continued to make swords for those daimyō who had kept a military outlook during the years of peace. The Satsuma swords are robust broad blades, owing much to the Sōshū style, with large nie and characteristic long kinsuji throughout the hamon.

Yoshimune commissioned the Honami to compile a list of famous blades in the fourth year of the Kyōhō era, 1719, the *Kyōhō Meibutsu Chō*. The book is valuable evidence of the tastes of the daimyō at the time, indicating the collecting pattern of the Momoyama period. Swords of the Sōshū school are prominent, probably reflecting the Honami family history of cutting down swords of the Nambokuchō period, among which many were attested as being made by the pupils of Masamune. The most desirable blades were those made by Masamune and his pupils, although every daimyō also hoped to acquire a tantō by Awataguchi Yoshimitsu, or one of the Heian period masters like Munechika.

The late Edo period

Japan had remained isolated from foreign intercourse since the beginning of the Edo period, except for the activities of Dutch and Chinese trading-stations at Nagasaki.

However, around the end of the eighteenth century the appearance in Japanese waters of American, Russian and British ships brought about a resurgence of interest in other countries and at the same time the stirrings of an intense patriotic movement. There was dissatisfaction with the rigid Tokugawa system of government and a growing feeling of respect for the position of the Emperor, who still maintained the unbroken line in Kyoto even though real power was vested in the Shogun.

The revival in nationalistic spirit was accompanied by a revivalist movement in cultural areas. The *Kyōhō Meibutsu Chō* (see p. 14) was followed by a number of studies on swords. A swordsmith, Suishinshi Masahide (1750–1825), advocated a return to the traditions of the ancient schools. He and his many pupils strove to duplicate the work of the 'Five Traditions' of Bizen, Yamashiro, Yamato, Sōshū and Mino, most of them working in Bizen and Sōshū style. The shapes of their blades followed two main styles, the Kambun shintō and the Momoyama, based on the shape of the cut-down swords of the Kamakura and Nambokuchō periods. These swords are known as *shinshintō*, or 'new, new swords'. A little later than Masahide, Yamaura Kiyomaro (no. 78) of Shinshū Province specialised in Sōshū style, and particularly that of Shizu. His blades are majestic, both elegant in form and perfect in forging. Swordmaking was revived throughout the country, and smiths prospered: in Edo there was Masahide and his pupils, Naotane and Hosokawa Masayoshi; Kiyomaro had two great pupils, Kurihara Nobuhide and Kiyondo; Bizen-style swords were made by Ishidō Korekazu and Koyama Munetsugu; the ancient Gassan tradition was revived by Sadakatsu. In Kyūshū Motohira of Satsuma and Masayuki of Hōki made blades of robust proportions, and in Bizen the Yokoyama school made large swords with distinct nioi in chōji hamon.

After some considerable internal strife Japan recommenced trade with the nations which had been rejected for so long. Imperial rule was restored in 1867, and Western customs avidly absorbed. In 1876 a law prohibiting the wearing of swords in public was confirmed, thus bringing to an end a custom which had lasted since the days of the first Shogun at Kamakura, and symbolising the indisputable end of samurai government.

Nowadays the sword is recognised in Japan primarily as a work of art, and there are still many active smiths producing fine swords in both old and new styles. Some work in a conservative tradition, tracing their lineage back over many generations, and others have devoted their lives, like Suishinshi Masahide, to the quest to recover the secrets of the old masters who produced the finest swords in the world.

Sword-fittings

In the Edo period the Bakufu (p. 39) retained families of all manner of craftsmen who went to Edo to live and work. Their sword-fittings makers included the Gotō family, together with Inaba Yoshioka no Suke and Hirata Hikoshirō of Higo Province. These sponsored metalworkers, or *iebori* ('house carvers'), continued with their traditional designs to supply the demand for daishō according to the Tokugawa regulations.

The daishō meant a matching pair of swords. Usually this would apply to the lacquered scabbards, the hilt binding and the metal fittings. The *katana* (long sword) length was fixed at about 70 cm, and the wakizashi at about 50 cm. The hilts were to be bound with braids criss-crossing over in the manner known as *makikake*, and the binding had to be black. The fuchi had to be of the black patinated alloy of copper and gold, shakudō. The *kashira*, or pommel fitting, had to be of horn. The tsuba was to be polished black shakudō, but this regulation was not strictly applied. The midokoromono were to be made by the Gotō school (see p. 60, nos 108, 109). The metal pieces were to bear the mon of the owner's clan. The tip of the wakizashi scabbard had to be rounded. The daishō was also sometimes called *banzashi* ('duty wear'), or kamishimo zashi.

In the free spirit of the times an increasing demand for decorative work inspired independent studios to adventure with new alloys, designs and methods of manufacture. These studios, which came to be known as *machibori* ('town carvers'), produced fuchi and kashira, in addition to tsuba and midokoromono. Sets of fuchi and kashira provided an ideal vehicle for pictorial sculpture. Since they were separated by the length of the hilt, and since their surfaces were perpendicularly opposed, they could be used to express different aspects of any one theme. For example, the kashira is often used to depict a close view of a subject treated at a distance on the fuchi.

The most celebrated of the machibori artists, Yokoya Sōmin (1670–1733), had left the Gotō school dissatisfied with their required repetition of traditional themes. He treated the old subject-matter with an entirely fresh approach. One of his greatest contributions to the art of the decorative metalworker was *katakiri bori*, a method of engraving designs with oblique cuts of a triangular-pointed chisel which varied in width, depth and angle to simulate the brush lines in ink painting. From around this time metalworkers often carved designs from preliminary sketches provided by the great painters of the day, for the machibori artists were required to provide pictures in metal as realistic as any painting.

Sōmin's pupils, Sōyō II, Ōmori Eishō, Yoshikawa Genshin, Yanagawa Naomasa and Yokoya Eisei established their own independent studios, and their lineage can be followed for several generations. From the Yanagawa emerged the Ishiguro school and Kono Haruaki who was to achieve the Buddhist title of Hōgen.

Three contemporaries of Sōmin in Edo, Nara Toshinaga (d. 1737), Sugiura Jōi (d. 1751) and Tsuchiya Yasuchika (d. 1744), have become known as the *Nara san saku* ('three makers of the Nara school'). Jōi specialised in *shishiai bori*, or carving in sunken relief, often using the newly fashionable alloy *shibuichi* (literally one part in four), a mixture of a fourth part of silver in copper which could be patinated to a range of silvery greys and browns. Yasuchika was a master of inlay and has left many fine tsuba. In his old age he took the tonsure and adopted the Buddhist name Tōu, passing the name Yasuchika on to the second generation. Toshinaga specialised in shallow-relief sculpture on fuchi/kashira sets and has left few tsuba. A pupil of Toshinaga, Hamano Shōzui, was the first of several artists who sculpted the popular culture of Edo on fuchi/kashira and tsuba. A recurring theme of the school is scenes from the Chinese 'Tale of Three Kingdoms'. Other schools developed including those of Ichinomiya Nagatsune, Ōtsuki Mitsuyoshi, and in Mito Province the later Shōami, Ichiyanagi Tomoyoshi, Hagidani Katsuhira, and Egawa Toshimasa.

Among the last of the machibori artists in the nineteenth century was Kanō Natsuo (1828–98), who eventually became in the Meiji period a professor in the Tokyo School of Art and was awarded the distinction of being made a Craftsman of the Imperial Household. After the Meiji Restoration Natsuo led the movement for preserving the traditional techniques of the sword-fittings maker by encouraging purely ornamental sculpture. Gotō Ichijō (1791–1876) left many pieces of sword furniture in original style quite different from the iebori of his ancestors, often working in iron, in addition to the traditional shakudō. He passed his skill on to a number of pupils, much of whose work was never mounted on swords and can be frequently found in pristine condition in Western collections.

Horimono

The decorative tendency of the Momoyama period developed into more and more extravagant sculpture during the middle of the seventeenth century. The range of subject-matter grew to include purely auspicious themes, like the 'Three Friends', pine, plum and bamboo. In place of the ancient kurikara, dragons can be found wound around flowering plum boughs. Those deities who had been gods of war during the Muromachi period appear as gods of fortune. The symbol of the annual boys' festival, a carp ascending a waterfall, fills great panels in the blades.

The work of Ikkanshi Tadatsuna of Osaka during the peaceful Genroku era at the end of the seventeenth century was especially revered for both the quality of the blades and the excellence of his carving. He sometimes inscribed the words *hori dōsaku* on his tangs, to signify that he had made the horimono himself, for in busy times it was not unnatural for a swordsmith to obtain help with such demanding work. Tadatsuna made many wakizashi, and it is probable that the embellishment of horimono on

them would have earned him high prices among a merchant-class clientele in Osaka. In contrast, not many years before, Kotetsu of Edo had stopped carving horimono and having cutting tests inscribed on his tangs, perhaps because he had made for himself sufficient reputation, or in his maturity he felt that fashionable decoration was detrimental to the dignity of the sword.

After around half a century or so of decline in swordmaking, the revivalist shinshintō smiths of the middle eighteenth century began to make swords in both the Kambun shintō and kotō styles of the 'Five Traditions'. Their horimono were either decorative in Kambun style, or in the simple religious manner of the ancient styles.

Armour

Many styles of armour remained in use in the peaceful Edo period. Some samurai continued to take serviceable armour on their annual journeys to and from the capital, and others had lighter and comfortable armour made. Armourers made fine iron pieces, with suji kabuto formed of large numbers of plates, as many as sixty-two and sometimes more than a hundred, for their clients rejoiced in fine workmanship even though it had little practical justification. Many daimyō and other high-ranking samurai had armour made in ancient style, or had fine old helmets and other pieces remounted in new sets of armour. These revivalist ōyoroi continued to be made up until the nineteenth century, while the Sankin Kotai system continued to provide justification for its use.

Although armour has not been used in battle since the Meiji Restoration, an ongoing programme for reproducing and conserving important early pieces using traditional materials has ensured that the technology of manufacture at least has not been lost.

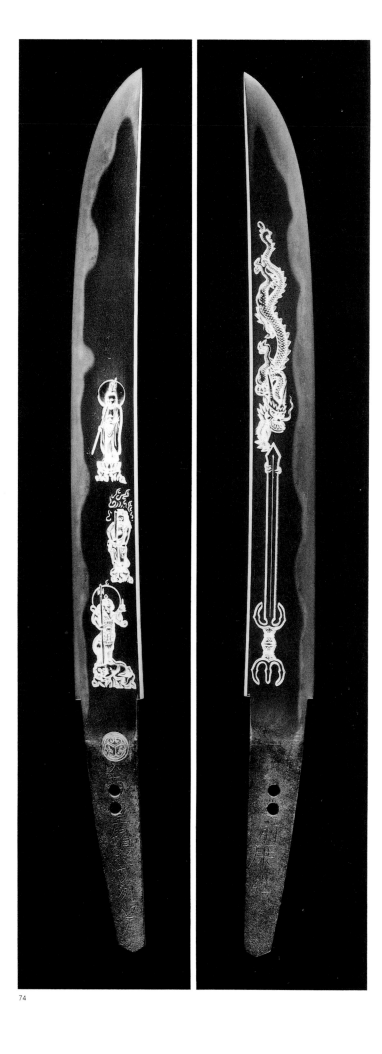

74 Wakizashi blade

Edo period, *c.* 1630
Signed: Echizen Yasutsugu (Yasutsugu II of
    Echizen, d. 1646) with inscription Motte
    Namban Tetsu Oite Bushū Edo ('Made with
    foreign steel in Edo, Bushū Province') and
    triple hollyhock leaf mon of Tokugawa family
L. 34.9 cm
Tokyo National Museum

This hira zukuri-type wakizashi blade is
decorated with carvings by Tomosuke of
the Kinai school, whose name is inscribed as
the carver of a very similar wakizashi dated
1630. One side of the blade carries a dragon
grasping the ritual vajra-hilted ken-type
sword, and the other has three Buddhist
deities: at the top the Bodhisattva Jizō with
canopy and treasure jewel, next the King of
Light, Fudō Myō-Ō, and at the bottom the
guardian deity, Bishamon.

The jihada is itame, and the hamon notare
in nie with midare, consciously emulating
the work of Masamune and Sadamune.
Yasutsugu II, like his father Yasutsugu I
(p. 89), worked in Edo for the Tokugawas
and also in Echizen Province for the
Matsudaira clan. The school continued for
several generations into the shinshintō
period.

Around 1634 Yasutsugu II entered the lay
priesthood, and his blades accordingly carry
the title Nyūdō ('he who has entered upon
the Way'), although the earliest known
example is dated 1637. He was well loved
by the Shogun Tokugawa Ietada, who gave
him a mansion in Kanda. He died in 1646.

75 Katana blade *(see also front cover)*

Edo period, 17th century
Signed: Omi no Kami Takagi Jū Sukenao
  ('Sukenao, with the honorary title Omi no
  Kami, living at Takagi')
L. 71.2 cm
British Museum, JA 1958, 7–30, 67. Bequeathed
  by R. W. Lloyd

The blade is of the Kambun era (1661–73)
shape (see also no. 76) reflecting the
development of formal indoor kendō
schools during the Edo period. Very showy
hamon were popular especially in Osaka
around the middle of the seventeenth
century, perhaps owing to the taste of the
largely merchant population of the city,
who were allowed to carry a wakizashi. The
tōran pattern of the hamon, in the form of
billowing waves, was established by Tsuda
Echizen no Kami Sukehiro, father of this
smith. The jigane of this perfectly forged
sword is a bright close itame, and the hamon
is rich in large nie crystals.

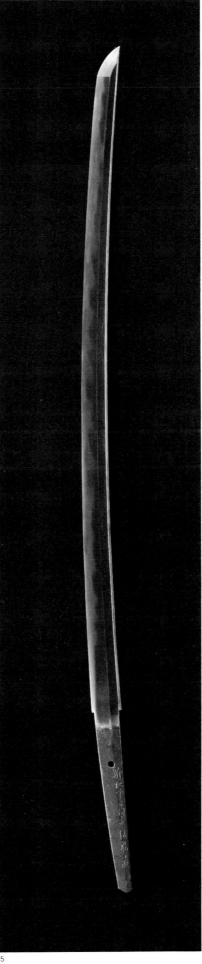

75

76 Katana blade *(illus. on p. 120)*

Edo period, c. 1672
Signed: Jū Tōeizan Shinobu ga Oka no Hotori
  Nagasone Tora Nyūdō ('Resident in Tōeizan
  Temple, Shinobu ga Oka no hitori [a place
  name] Nagasone [school name] Tora ['Tiger']
  Nyūdō [title for one having entered the
  priesthood]'). Nagasone Kotetsu, c. 1605–78
L. 75.4 cm
Sword Museum, Tokyo

This blade is of the typical Kambun shintō
shape, with a shallow curve and narrowing
towards the kissaki (see also no. 75). The
jigane is tightly packed itame, flowing in
places, bright with delicate jinie and chikei.
The hamon is of long shallow notare mixed
with gunome, deep in nioi with konie and
the broad ashi characteristic of the smith's
work. Also characteristic of Kotetsu is the
gently sloping yakidashi and the komaru
boshi which swells slightly downwards in a
rounded form described as resembling the
pad of a man's thumb.
  Originally an armour maker of Echizen,
Kotetsu went to Edo at the age of fifty-one
in 1656 to embark upon a career as
swordsmith. He used three different
characters to write the name 'Kotetsu' at
different periods of his life, so his works
may be fairly accurately dated. Kotetsu was
a horimono artist of great skill, although he
did not carve on his late works. His hamon
include many suguha, in his early period a
form of double gunome known as *hyōtan ba*
(*hyōtan* – a double gourd), and in his later
life the regular form of rounded gunome
known as juzuba.

77 Katana blade *(illus. on p. 121)*

Edo period, 17th century
Signed: Tatara Chōkō, Oite ('in') Settsu Kuni
  ('Province') kore o tsukuru ('made this'), with
  gold inscription Mitsodō kiriotoshi ('cut
  through three bodies together') and further
  painted vermilion-lacquered inscription
  Omigami Ason Kanjo Shōji
L. 68.2 cm

This broad blade is in the style of a cut-
down Nambokuchō period tachi of
immense proportions. The jigane is itame
with some jinie, and the hamon is a vigorous
large gunome pattern in Sue Bizen style.
  Chōkō, or Nagayoshi, was one of the
Ishido group (p. 114) of Edo period smiths
who worked in the Bizen style, sometimes
producing large and expressive chōji hamon
similar to Kamakura period work. This
sword was carried in the Meiji period by
General Tani Kanjo.

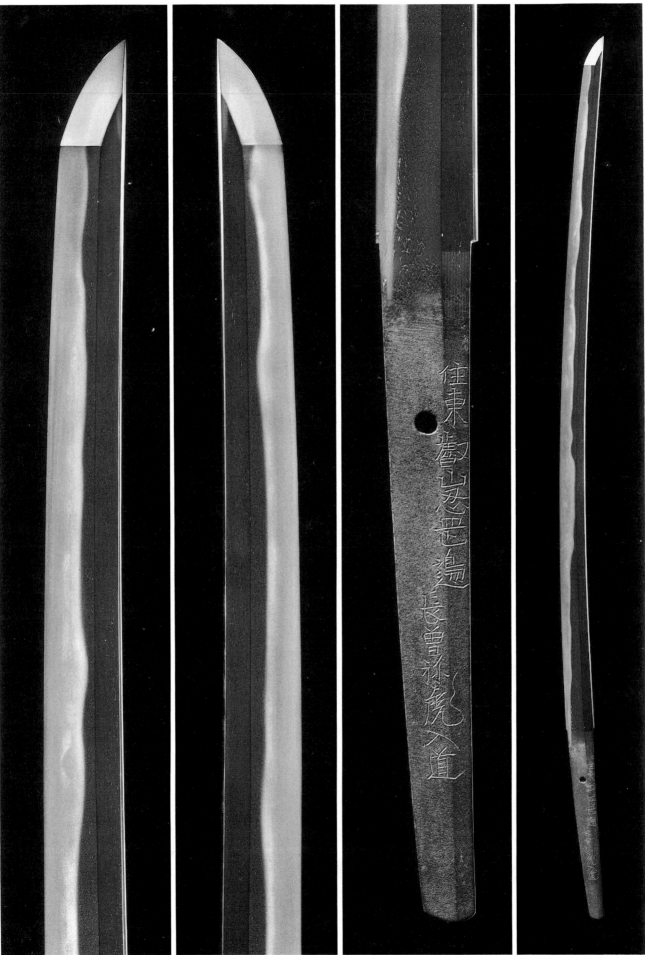

大神朝臣一城所持
参陸集國作之

多々良長茟
三ッ胴切落

三胴切落

源清麿

嘉永元年八月日

78 Daishō *(illus. on pp. 122–3)*

Dated: Kaei gannen hachi gatsu hi (a day in
August 1848)
Signed: Minamoto Kiyomaro
L. (katana) 68.4 cm; (wakizashi) 48.2 cm

Both swords are in the broad, long-pointed
shape of shinshintō in the style of
Momoyama period blades and cut-down
swords of the Nambokuchō period. The
grain is a flowing large itame, and with large
jinie and chikei. The hamon is bright
gunome midare with small notare, and with
ashi, coarse patches of nie and sunagashi.
The boshi is midare style, with a komaru
return and some hakikake. Both blades have
broad bohi grooves, the hira zukuri
construction wakizashi also with soehi.

Kiyomaro was born in Komoro of
Shinshū Province, and studied at first with
his brother Saneo under Kawamura
Toshitaka, a retainer of the Ueda family. At
one time he used the name Hidetoshi, and
later changed it to Masayuki. In 1844 he
went to Edo to study military strategy and
continue swordmaking. In 1846 he assumed
the name Kiyomaro. Of all the late Edo
period smiths his work follows the Sōshū
tradition most closely. A comparison of
these two blades with the swords by the
Sōshū school smiths Masamune and
Sadamune (nos 24, 25) made 500 years
before well illustrates the difference between
kotō and shinshintō revivalist blades.

79 Katana blade

Dated: Meiji nijū nana nen jūni gatsu hi (a day in
December 1893)
Signed: Osaka Jū Gassan Sadakatsu Seitan kore
('finely forged by Gassan Sadakatsu resident
in Osaka') with inscription horimono dō saku
('carving made by the same man')
L. 71.5 cm
Tokyo National Museum

The grain of this blade is itame but flowing
almost wholly into masame, with jinie. The
hamon is notare with gunome, deep nioi and
nie with sunagashi. The boshi is midare with
pointed hakikake. The carving on one side
is of a plum kurikara, in which the plum
bough takes the place of Fudō Myō-Ō's
sword. The other side has Fudō Myō-Ō
standing in flames, and a single groove
extending from above the deity.

Gassan Sadakatsu was the adopted son of
Sadayoshi, who had been born in Dewa
Province, home of the Gassan tradition, the
son of Gassan Yasaburō Sadachika.
Sadakatsu's swordmaking career met a
setback with the prohibition of wearing
swords after the Meiji Restoration, but he
continued despite the adverse situation to
become appointed in 1905 to the
distinguished position of Craftsman to the
Imperial Household. Sadakatsu died in 1918,
having kept alive the long tradition of the
Gassan school with the distinctive ayasugi
sinusoidal grain pattern, and having
produced works also in the ancient styles of
Bizen, Sōshū and Yamato. His carvings
emulated the work of the seventeenth-
century swordsmith Ikkanshi Tadatsuna.

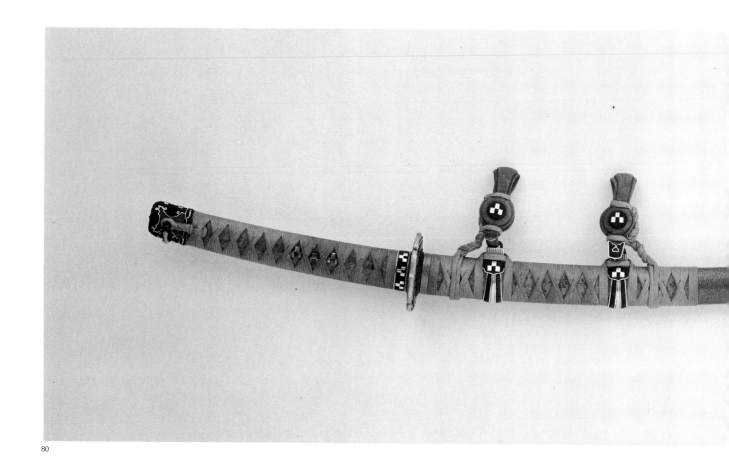

80

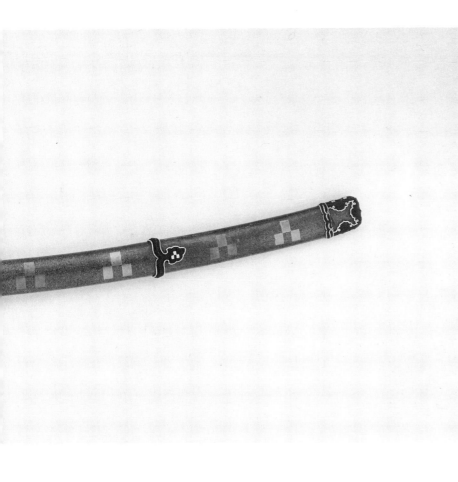

80 Ito maki tachi mounting

Edo period, 18th century
L. 97.2 cm
British Museum, JA 1958, 7–30, 149. Given by
    R. W. Lloyd

The gold-lacquered ito maki tachi, made for
wear with armour, was carried during the
Edo period by daimyō and other high-
ranking persons when travelling with their
retinues to and from the capital. The metal
pieces on this rich mounting bear the triple
paving-stone mon of the Tsuchiya family of
the Tsuchiura clan, inlaid in gold on a
shakudō nanako ground, and the same mon
is repeated in gold foil on the lacquered
scabbard.

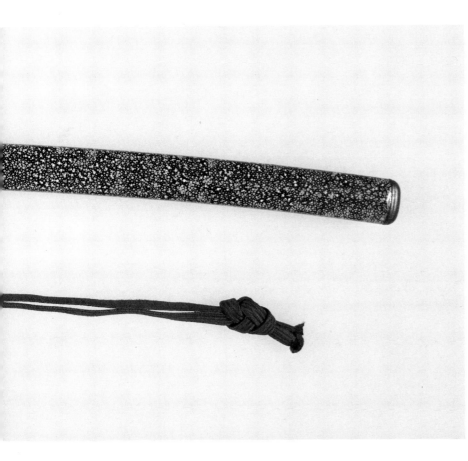

81 Uchigatana mounting

Edo period, 18th century
L. 93.2 cm

The scabbard is of black-lacquered and
polished ray-fish skin. The hilt is bound with
leather over menuki in the form of fruits
made of shakudō with gold inlay. The kōgai
and kozuka are carved with waves in
shakudō. The tsuba, of red copper with a
fukurin of shakudō, is in the *namako* ('sea
cucumber') form introduced by Miyamoto
Musashi (nos 100, 105, 106). This is a Higo-
type mounting, with a rounded kashira and
kojiri ('chape'), characteristic serviceable
tsuba and hilt bound with leather.

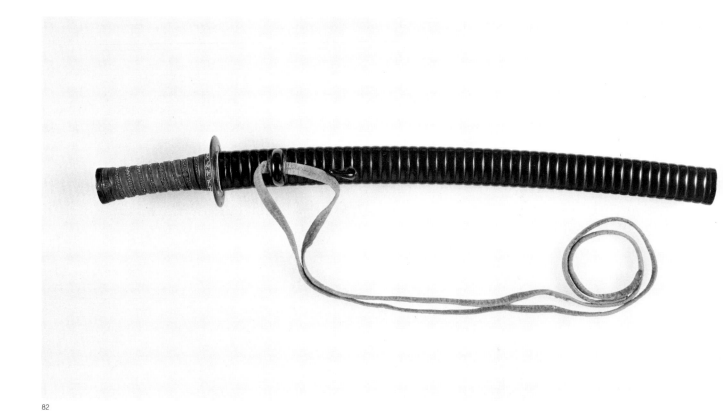

82

82 Koshigatana mounting

Edo period, 17th century
L. 58.6 cm

The scabbard is of finest-quality black-ribbed
lacquerwork. Although the hilt is bound
with a single helical strip of leather thong,
quite different from the prescribed fashion,
the kashira is of horn in keeping with official
regulations. The fuchi has auspicious
emblems inlaid in gold on a shakudō nanako
ground.

Both the mounting and the blade (no. 36)
once belonged to the swordsman Yagyū
Munenori, whose school of kendō included
the Tokugawa Shoguns among its devotees.

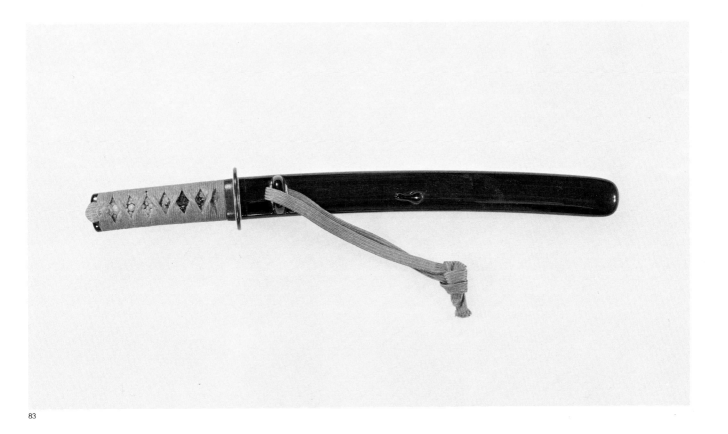

83

83 Wakizashi mounting

Edo period, 17th–18th century
Signed (kozuka): Kenjō and Mitsutoshi with
 maker's mark; attributed to Gotō Kenjō by
 Gotō Mitsutoshi (1663–1721)
L. 49.5 cm
Agency for Cultural Affairs, Tokyo, Important
 Cultural Property

This is the mounting for the Ishida
Sadamune tantō (no. 25). It is in kamishimo
regulation style, black-lacquered with a horn
kashira, shakudō nanako fuchi, and shakudō
tsuba and menuki. The kozuka is decorated
with salmon and bamboo grass.

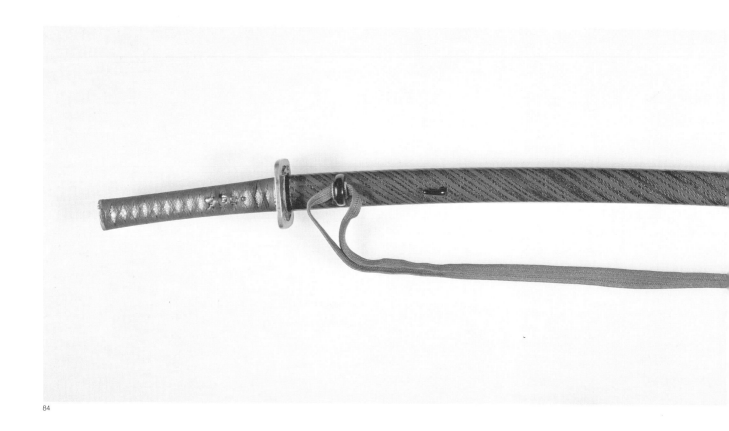

84

85

84 Uchigatana mounting

Edo period, 18th century
Signed (tsuba): Yasuchika, with seal on other metal
    pieces. Tsuchiya Yasuchika II (1695–1747)
L. 96.0 cm
Sword Museum, Tokyo

The hilt of this colourful mounting is
wrapped with white ray-fish skin and bound
with brown-lacquered wisteria rattan. The
menuki are in the form of horses of warmly
patinated copper with tails and manes
detailed in gold inlay. The fuchi/kashira
have shells and paulownia mon inlaid in
gold, shakudō and copper on a shinchū
ground (see also no. 129).

  The tsuba is of shinchū, a round-cornered
square form with Chōkarō and two horses
having issued from his gourd roundly carved
in openwork with various inlaid metals and
line engraving. The scabbard is decorated
with helical bands of vermilion lacquer and
silver strip over a black-lacquered ray-fish
skin patterned ground. The blade for this
mounting is an unsigned cut-down tachi
attributed to the fourteenth-century smith
Samonji of Chikuzen Province, a fitting
sword for this finest-quality work of
Yasuchika. The sword was carried by the
distinguished statesman of the Meiji period
who developed the Sahalin islands north of
Hokkaidō, Kuroda Kiyotaka.

85 Mounting for daishō

(illus. in colour on p. 82)

Edo period, 18th century
Signed (fuchi/kashira): Nomura Masayuki
L. (katana) 93.9 cm; (wakizashi) 70.4 cm

The scabbards of this matching pair of
swords are wrapped with ray-fish skin
lacquered blue overall, polished down to
reveal the fish-skin in butterfly shapes in the
natural white of the material, with gold
pigment. The fuchi and kashira are
decorated with the Tanabata Festival theme
(see no. 110) in high-relief inlay on a
shakudō nanako ground. The
midokoromono, by Gotō Teijō (1603–73),
are of shells with gold inlay on shakudō.
The matching tsuba are decorated with
insects on a copper nanako ground.

86 Mounting for daishō

Edo period, 19th century
L. (katana) 88.7 cm; (wakizashi) 63.0 cm
Sword Museum, Tokyo

This pair of swords are mounted in standard
kamishimo style for official wear. The
kashira are of horn, and the other small metal
fittings of shakudō nanako ground, with the
gold-inlaid mon of the Nabeshima clan of
Hizen Province. Few daishō mountings
have survived in such perfect condition.

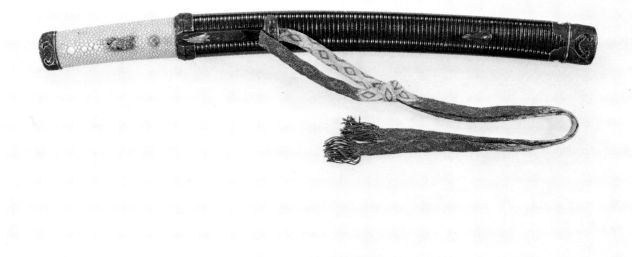

87

87 Aikuchi mounting

Edo period, 19th century
L. 53.5 cm
Tokyo National Museum

As an accessory this mounting embodies the sophisticated fashion of the Edo period. The scabbard is lacquered in nashiji style, with gold particles shining from beneath the surface. The broad ribbed shape is known as *inrō kizami* ('sculpted seal box'), since it resembles the set of sliding compartments of an inrō. The metal fittings are by the master Gotō Ichijō, with gold menuki in the form of a phoenix and a kirin (mythical beast with lion's tail, cloven hooves and dragon's scales), and with a turtle and a dragon on the kōgai and the kozuka respectively, in gold inlay on shakudō sculpted on a shakudō nanako ground. Such minute particles of nanako are one of the marks of Ichijō's work. The other metal fittings are decorated with waves carved in high relief in shakudō against a nanako ground, with edging in gold.

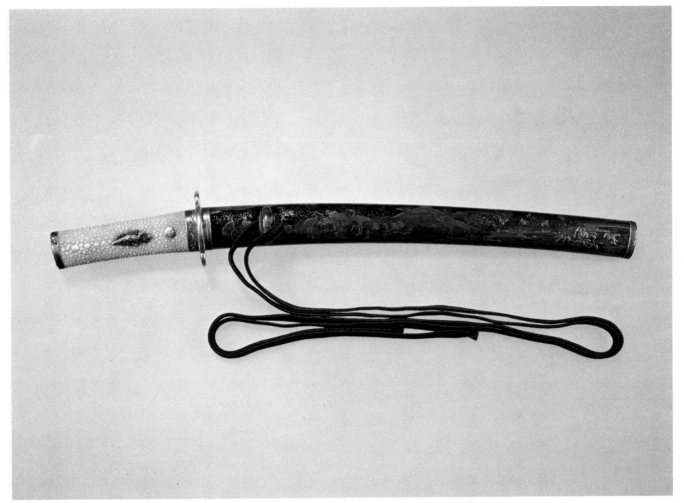

88

88 Tsuba katana mounting

Edo period, 19th century
L. (overall) 55.1 cm
Tokyo National Museum

From the Kamakura to the Edo period short swords and their mountings were known as koshigatana. In the Edo period those with tsuba were called tsuba katana, or *chisa* ('small') katana, and mountings without a tsuba were called aikuchi (see no. 87).

This piece is a tsuba katana of the late Edo period. The tsuba, kozuka, fuchi/kashira and other small metal parts are charmingly inlaid with peafowl and other birds and flowers, and can be reliably attributed to the work of Gotō Ichijō. The scabbard is worked in gold and coloured makie with the cranes and pines of Hōraizan (the Chinese Island of Immortality), with a bright red sun and a Hōraizan hinting at Mount Fuji, both fitting for the nationalistic spirit of the last days of the Shogunate.

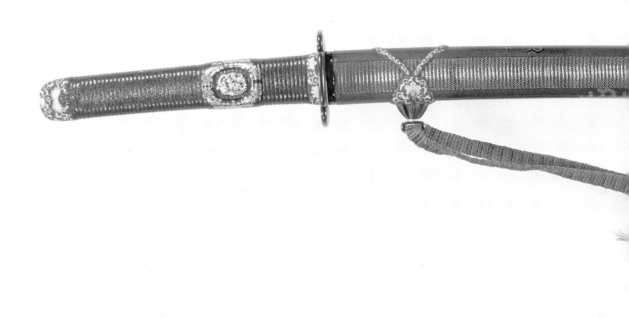

89

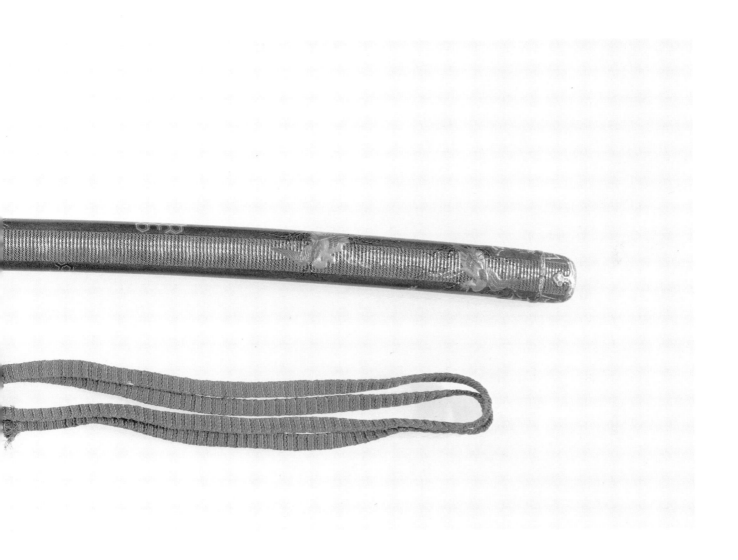

89 Uchigatana mounting

Edo period, 19th century
L. 98.0 cm

An elegant uchigatana mounting with
scabbard of lacquered ray-fish skin, and with
the two edges of the scabbard lacquered in
black *ishime* ('stone grain') in imitation of
metal rims. The scabbard has phoenixes in
high-relief gold lacquer, and the metal
pieces are shakudō with gold paulownia
mon and foliage in level inlay.

The sword is displayed on a Meiji period
mulberry-wood tachi stand of the
nineteenth century.

90 Efu tachi mounting

(illus. in colour on pp. 110–11)

Edo period, 19th century
L. 97.7 cm
Tokyo National Museum

This style of ceremonial mounting is named
after the *efu*, or palace guards, who carried
it. The gold ikakeji lacquer scabbard bears
the Imperial chrysanthemum, and the metal
fittings, except for the shakudō of the tsuba,
are richly gilded. The hilt of the efu tachi is
always clad with metal strips along both
edges. Since the Kamakura period the
menuki have been in the tweezer shape of
the hilts of early Heian period kenuki gata
tachi. The sword came from the family of
the late Prince Takamatsu.

91 *enlarged by 30%*

91 Tsuba

Iron, pierced in positive silhouette with broken bamboo

Edo period, 17th century
Unsigned; attributed to Matashichi of Higo
    Province
H. 7.8 cm

The bamboo represents resilience under pressure and is often used as a military motif. A broken bamboo perhaps indicates the sad nobility of failure.

Hayashi Matashichi was the founder of the Kasuga school of Higo Province under the patronage of the Hosokawa daimyōs.

92 *enlarged by 30%*

92 Tsuba

Iron, pierced in positive and negative silhouette with *kuyō* and cherry mon

Edo period, 17th century
Unsigned; attributed to Matashichi of Higo
    Province
H. 7.8 cm

The two designs are reproduced to startling effect. Both the *kuyō* ('nine stars') and cherry blossom mon were used by the Hosokawa daimyō under whose patronage Matashichi worked.

93 Tsuba *(illus. in colour on p. 106)*

Iron, pierced in positive silhouette with encircled crane

Edo period, 17th century
Unsigned; attributed to Matashichi of Higo
    Province
H. 8.5 cm

The auspicious crane is found in many forms symbolising longevity. This rounded 'dancing crane' design has been used widely since the time of Matashichi both on tsuba and as a decoration on textiles and lacquerware.

94 Tsuba

Iron, pierced in positive and negative silhouette with drifting cherry blossoms

Edo period, 17th century
Unsigned; attributed to Matashichi of Higo
    Province
H. 8.0 cm

Matashichi's clever use of both positive and negative silhouette contains an allusion to the cherry as a symbol of the spirit of the samurai, since the flower falls from the tree suddenly while still in full bloom, as the warrior is required to die at a moment in the fullness of youth in the service of his lord.

94   *enlarged by 30%*

95 *enlarged by 30%*

95 Tsuba

Iron, pierced in positive silhouette with *yatsuhashi* bridge motif

Edo period, 18th century
Unsigned; attributed to Tōhachi of Higo Province
(1711–79)
H. 7.9 cm

The *yatsuhashi* bridge is depicted below clouds with finely engraved irises. The bridge consists of a number of short flat sections laid in a zigzag fashion across ponds or small streams. With irises, the bridge alludes to an event in the life of Ariwara no Narihira recorded in the classic tenth-century *Ise Monogatari* ('Tales of Ise'). Tōhachi specialised in the cherry and kuyō design, and sometimes copied the work of Matashichi, signing his pieces 'Hayashi Tōhachi, the third generation after Matashichi'.

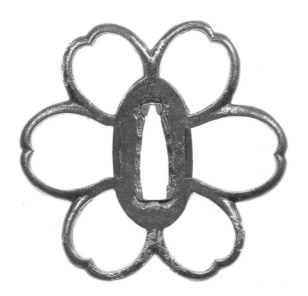

96 Tsuba

Iron, pierced in positive and negative silhouette in the form of cherry blossom

Edo period, 17th century
Unsigned; attributed to Nishigaki Kanjirō
(1613–93)
H. 7.9 cm

97 Tsuba

Iron, pierced in positive silhouette with
paulownia by window, with rim in
outline of stylised chrysanthemum
blossom

Edo period, 17th century
Unsigned; attributed to Nishigaki Kanjirō (1st of
   3 generations, 1613–93)
H. 8.0 cm

97   enlarged by 30%

98 Tsuba

Iron, pierced in positive silhouette with
willow and stylised heron

Edo period, 18th century; Akasaka school
H. 8.1 cm

98   enlarged by 30%

99   *enlarged by 30%*

99 Tsuba

Iron, pierced in positive silhouette with
bows and arrows facing four directions

Edo period, 17th century; Akasaka school
H. 8.5 cm

The theme usually represents Hachiman,
Shintō patron of archers, and is sometimes
found together with written invocations to
the deity.

100 *enlarged by 30%*

100 Tsuba

Iron, pierced in negative silhouette
with namako

Edo period, 17th century
Unsigned; attributed to Miyamoto Musashi
  (1584–1645)
H. 7.5 cm

This most simple of motifs is believed to
have been sculpted by the hand of the
'sword saint', Musashi, some time after his
enlightenment at the age of fifty. From 1640
until the end of his life he enjoyed the
sponsorship of the Hosokawa family in
Higo Province, and spent his time in
teaching kendō and professing all manner
of arts and crafts (see also no. 105).

101 Tsuba

Iron, pierced in positive silhouette
with triangle and three spheres

Edo period, 17th century; Yagyū school
H. 8.0 cm

This type of tsuba is said to derive from the
taste of the swordsman Yagyū Renyasai
Toshikane (1625–94) of the Shinkage school
of kendō. Very much in the robust style of
the Owari and Kanayama schools, many of
the pieces, like this one, carry motifs
connected with the philosophy of kendō.
This motif is usually described as 'three
stars', but the triangular form might
represent the Shingon Buddhism concept
sanshō, meaning the seed, maturity and effect
of the Buddhist law. The three spheres could
then indicate the past, present and future
worlds, the unity of cause and effect which
is central also to the moon and waves design
(no. 103).

102 Tsuba

Iron, pierced in positive silhouette
with single bamboo

Edo period, 17th century; Yagyū school
H. 7.4 cm

Bamboo is a favourite motif of the
swordsman, representing both resilience and
strength. Bamboo was used by kendō
schools for their practice swords, and the
single bamboo might with some imagination
be interpreted as the central teaching of the
Yagyū school, *itto ryōdan*, the ultimate cut
in perfect accord with the opponent's attack.

103 Tsuba

Iron, pierced and roundly carved with
moon and waves

Edo period, 17th century; Yagyū school
H. 7.1 cm

The moon is reflected in untroubled water
without plan or effort in accordance with
nature, like the swordsman's response to his
opponent's actions. This concept was
revealed to Yagyū Tajima no Kami
Munenori in the early seventeenth century
by the Zen priest Takuan.

103   *enlarged by 30%*

104 Tsuba

Iron, pierced in positive silhouette
with a pine

Edo period, 18th century; Tosa Myōchin school
H. 8.2 cm

This is the work of armourers of the
Myōchin family living in Tosa Province,
who made iron tsuba during the late Edo
period. They were influenced by the
Akasaka school of Edo, and their work
displays the imaginative artistry of the
Akasaka makers together with the powerful
lines natural to a long and confident
tradition of iron armour makers.

104   *enlarged by 30%*

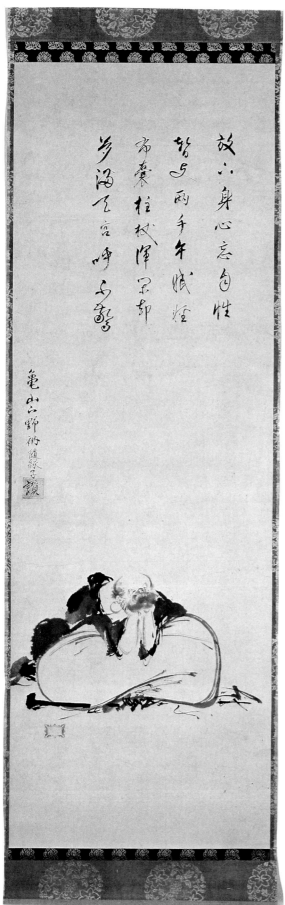

105 Hotei

Hanging scroll, ink on paper
c. 1635–45
Seal: Niten. Miyamoto Musashi (1584–1645)
110.5 × 38.0 cm
Sword Museum, Tokyo

Hotei was popularised in Japan as one of the Shichi Fukujin ('Seven Deities of Fortune'). He is said to have originally been a Chinese priest who kept all his belongings in a sack, from which his name derives (see also no. 109). He is often depicted together with mirthful Chinese children, with whom he is on excellent terms, and who sometimes ride in his sack. In his cheerful rotundity he represents the Zen concept of *jujitsu*, or 'fullness'. A remark attributed to him, that there was no place in the world for him to put his stick, exemplifies the principle of kendō expressed in the self-portrait of the artist (no. 106). For the enlightened person there is no *suki* ('gap') in his knowledge of the world, no chink in his armour. He will not be disturbed by any non-essential action.

The poem, which was added by the artist's friend Zuienshi, the 207th abbot of Tenryūji Temple in Kyoto, reads:

> The enlightened priest forgetting himself,
> Dozing at noon upon his two hands,
> Sack and stick are out of his thoughts,
> Dreaming in Heaven, even a shout will
> not surprise him.

106 Miyamoto Musashi
(1584–1645)

Portrait, ink and colours on paper
Edo period, 17th century
180.0 × 39.6 m

Miyamoto Musashi was one of the many
rōnin ('wave men'), samurai made masterless
upon the pacification of Japan by Tokugawa
Ieyasu, following the battle of Seki ga Hara
in 1603. Devoting his life to the study of
kendō, he became invincible in combat, and
was enlightened at around the age of fifty.
He spent the remainder of his days teaching
and practising all manner of arts and crafts.
His metalwork (no. 100), calligraphy, ink
painting (no. 105) and sculpture are all
highly regarded as the work of a master in
each field. Musashi spent his last years as
guest of Lord Hosokawa of Kumamoto
Castle in Higo Province, to die alone in the
cave known as Reigendō, having retired
there some months before. He is known as
kensei ('sword saint'). His treatise on kendō
Go Rin No Shō ('A Book of Five Rings'),
written just days before his death, remains
the ultimate authority on the subject.

   This version of what is believed to be a
self-portrait of Musashi shows him wielding
both swords in the fencing attitude *happo
biraki* ('open in all eight directions'), and
implies that there is no possible opening
whereby he might be successfully attacked.
Several copies of the painting exist, but this
one was handed down by the Terao family.
Terao Magonojō was the pupil to whom
Musashi addressed *Go Rin No Shō* just days
before his lonely death, and is thought to
be the earliest and most authentic.

106

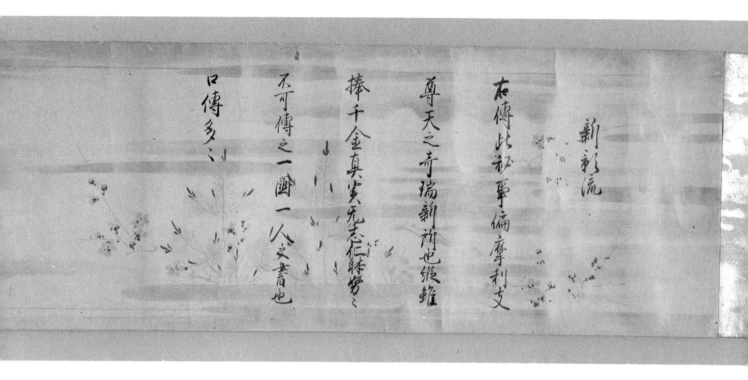

口傳多之

不可傳之一圖一人文書也

捧千金真實先志仁睦勞之

尊天之奇瑞新前也継雑

右傳此私軍偏摩利支

新新流

107 Yagyū Ryū Tengu Hiden Shō

Handscroll, ink and colours on paper
Dated: In accordance with 1752
Mitake Sanemon
18.5 × 527 cm

The 'Yagyū School Secret Traditions of the Tengu' illustrates the formal kendō exercises of the Shinkage school performed by the *tengu*, long-nosed winged mountain-dwelling creatures. Those of the Kurama mountains are said to have taught Minamoto Yoshitsune swordplay in his youth, and there are many other myths surrounding their sword-fencing prowess. The document is based on a treatise on kendō which was written in the form of a conversation between tengu, overheard by chance by a recluse.

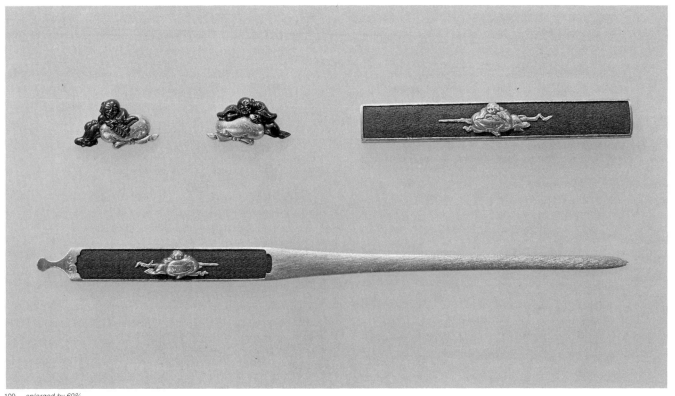

109　enlarged by 60%

108　Midokoromono

(illus. in colour on p. 86)

Decorated with scenes from Gempei wars in shakudō, gold and silver; on gilt kōgai high-relief inlay on shakudō nanako ground

Edo period, 17th century
Signed with attribution to Gotō Renjō (1628–1708) by Mitsuyoshi (1780–1843)
L. (kozuka) 9.5 cm

The theme is of the wars between the Taira and Minamoto (1180–5), ending in victory for the Minamoto and the establishment of the military government at Kamakura.

Gotō Shirōbei succeeded as the tenth generation of the Gotō school. He served the Tokugawa Shogun first in Yamashiro Province, and in 1662 moved the main family to Edo. In 1683 he entered the priesthood, taking the name Renjō, sometimes also signing Mitsutomo. Renjō instituted the custom of certifying the unsigned works of his ancestors, as his successor Mitsoyoshi did on this tsuba. He specialised in the depiction of human figures, birds, beasts and flowers in high-relief gold inlay on a ground of skakudō nanako.

109　Midokoromono

Decorated with Hotei in gold *suemon* inlay on shakudō nanako ground on kozuka and kōgai, which are gilded on undersides, and on menuki in gold inlay on shakudō

Edo period, 17th century
Signed: Gotō Kenjō (1586–1663) and with maker's mark
L. (kozuka) 9.6 cm

Hotei occurs frequently in popular Japanese art, being classed as one of the Shichi Fukujin ('Seven Deities of Fortune'; see also no. 105).

Kenjō, or Masatsugu, was the seventh head of the Gotō family. Around 1627, at the invitation of the Maeda family, he began to spend alternate years in Kaga, establishing the Kaga Gotō school. He made many kozuka, and also tsuba probably in response to the regulations governing the mountings of daisho for formal wear.

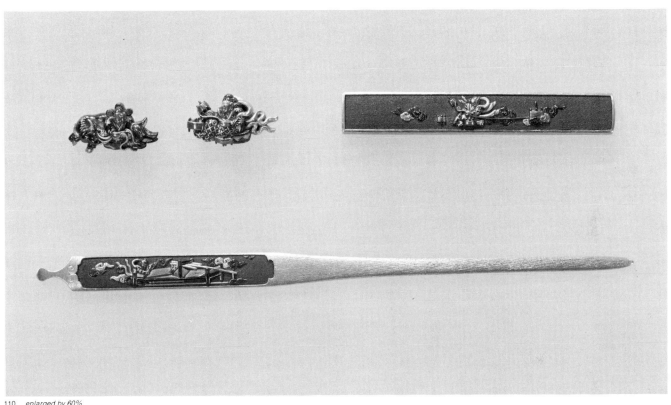

110   *enlarged by 60%*

110   Midokoromono

Decorated with herdsman and weaver girl in high-relief coloured-metal inlay on shakudō, with gilt kozuka and kōgai having panels of shakudō nanako

Edo period, 17th century
Signed: Gotō Mitsutomo (Renjō 1628–1708)
L. (kozuka) 9.7 cm

The king of heaven took pity on a weaving girl, who worked all day at her loom with no recreation, and introduced her to a cattle herdsman. The two fell in love, and the girl forsook her work. Their king was so angered that he decreed the two should be separated to meet on one day in the year. They became stars, separated by the Milky Way, and join annually on the Tanabata Festival of 7 July. On that day every family hangs paper priests on a tree, beseeching them to bring fine weather; for if just one drop of rain falls at Tanabata time, it will fill the whole of the Milky Way and the stars will not be able to meet.

111 *enlarged by 30%*

111 Tsuba

With gold fukurin, and decorated with horsemen racing before the *torii* gateway to Kamo Shrine in high-relief gold, copper and shakudō inlay on round shakudō nanako ground

Edo period, 17th century
Gotō Renjō (1628–1708, the 10th generation of the school) with appraisal inscription by Gotō Mitsuyoshi (1780–1843, the 15th generation)
H. 7.8 cm

There are a number of Kamo shrines in different parts of Japan, but the main one is that in Kyoto, founded in 678 in the reign of the Emperor Temmu. An annual festival instituted by the Emperor includes a festival procession and a wild horse race through the streets by armoured riders.

112 Menuki

Gold, two pairs of frolicking shishi

Edo period, 18h century
Unsigned; attributed to Yokoya Sōmin (1670–1733)
L. 3.6 cm, 3.8 cm

Generally recognised as the founder of the machibori movement, Sōmin studied under the painters Hanabusa Itchō and Kano Tanyū, who provided drawings of shishi, among other subjects, for the craftsman to work from. His pupils included Sōyō, who specialised in similar designs.

113 Set of fuchi/kashira and tsuba

(illus. in colour on p. 87)

Decorated with shishi and peonies in high-relief coloured-metal inlay on shakudō nanako ground with gold menuki of shishi

Edo period, 18th century
Signed: Sōyō on all pieces except kashira and with maker's mark. Yokoya Sōyō (1699–1779)
H. (tsuba) 7.9 cm; L. (fuchi) 4.1 cm; (kashira) 3.8 cm; (menuki) 3.5 cm

Often depicted among peonies, the shishi teaches its young to survive in a harsh world by dropping them over precipices, as depicted on the tsuba. The menuki represent the male and female principles yin and yang, that with the open mouth being the male, and always fixed on the side of the hilt which faces outwards when the sword is worn.

Sōyō was the pupil of Yokoya Sōmin (1670–1733). Much of his work is done with the katakiri bori style of engraving with oblique cuts of the chisel in simulation of brush strokes which he learned from Sōmin (no. 112), together with the lively designs of shishi, which are usually depicted together with the peony.

112

114

114 Menuki

Gold, decorated with monkeys as Sambasō dancers

Edo period, 18h century
Signed (inset gold tablets): Sōyō and with maker's mark
L. 2.4 cm

The Sambasō dance is performed by two actors in both the Nō and Kabuki theatres. They wear the masks of Okina, an old man, and carry fans and the ritual furiko wand of bells. One of the performers has a high hat with a representation of the sun on one side of it.

115   *enlarged by 30%*

115 Tsuba

Decorated with shishi and peonies in katakiri bori on polished patinated shibuichi ground

Edo period, 17th–18th century
Signed: Sōyō and with maker's mark
H. 7.4 cm

This familiar motif of the shishi and peonies illustrates Sōyō's skill in katakiri bori. The varying width of the chisel cut, the changes in its inclination, and the shadows and reflections inside the lines contrive together to produce the effect of ink painting. The same subject is treated by the artist using high-relief inlay in the tsuba, no. 113.

116   Tsuba *(illus. in colour on p. 108)*

Decorated with standing horses in high-relief shakudō suemon on shakudō nanako ground, with gold fukurin, and with opening for kozuka also rimmed with gold

Edo period, 18th century
Signed: Sōyō and with maker's mark
H. 7.8 cm

This elegant rendering is of a theme used by Sōyō's master, Sōmin, for menuki and on kozuka.

117 reverse, enlarged by 30%

117 Tsuba (illus. in colour on p. 109)

Decorated with attributes of Daikoku
and Ebisu in high-relief coloured-
metal suemon on fine ishime
hammered shakudō ground

Edo period, 18th century
Signed: Buyo Sanjin Kanshōdō Jōchiku and with
    gold inlaid seal on reverse. Murakami Jōchiku
    (d. *c.* 1800)
H. 7.5 cm

This tsuba is an example of the very typical
Japanese custom of expressing a theme
without the main component. Here the
popular deities of fortune, Daikoku and
Ebisu, are indicated by their attributes, the
sack of plenty and magic mallet of Daikoku,
and the sea bream and fishing line of Ebisu.
The eye of the bream is of shell inlay. The
character *kotobuki*, meaning 'felicitations' or
'longevity', is repeated around the rim of
the tsuba in gold inlay.

Little is known about the early life of
Murakami Jōchiku, although it has been said
that he originally did inlay work on stirrups.
His tsuba include highly decorative pieces,
with inlaid butterflies and other designs. He
specialised in *hira zogan* ('level inlay'), and
also used enamel and shell inlay. Jōchiku had
a number of pupils, one of whom succeeded
him in name, and whose technique is similar
to the skilful inlay of his master.

118 Tsuba

Iron, pierced and carved with Shōki
and demon in high-relief coloured-
metal inlay

Edo period, 18th century
Signed: Mito jū Michitoshi saku ('Made by Yatabe
    Michitoshi [1697–1768] of Mito')
H. 7.8 cm
Sword Museum, Tokyo

The bearded Chinese warrior Shōki, whose
eternal task is to purge the empire of
demons, is often depicted in pursuit armed
with his double-edged sword, or otherwise
nonplussed, being unable to spot their
hiding-place or determine their intention.

Michitoshi studied under various schools,
including the Nara school in Edo. He was
to a great extent the inspiration behind the
excellence of metalwork in Mito of Hitachi
Province, and excelled particularly in pierced
and roundly carved iron tsubas.

118   enlarged by 30%

120 *front*

120 *reverse*

119 **Pair of tsuba** *(illus. in colour on p. 111)*

Engraved with folding screens and fans and level-inlaid in gold, silver and shakudō on polished shibuichi ground

Edo period, 19th century
H. 8.1 and 7.7 cm

The metalworkers of Kaga were skilled in hira zogan, which was used to decorate guns, stirrups, various vessels and implements, and sword-fittings. Kaga zogan work of tsuba makers is often distinctive in that the outline of the inlay is marked by a clearly visible engraved line.

120 **Tsuba**

Ataka no seki in coloured-metal inlay on shibuichi ground

Edo period, 18th century
Signed: Hakuhotei Iwamoto Konkan (1744–1801)
and with maker's mark
H. 7.8 cm

This tsuba depicts the Kabuki drama *Kanjinchō* with Minamoto Yoshitsune as well as Benkei and other retainers in the garb of *yamabushi* ('mountain priests').

Miyamoto Yoshitsune, parted from his beloved wife, Shizuka, at Yoshino, had travelled far with his trusted retainer Benkei to escape from the forces of his brother, Yoritomo, together with a handful of retainers all disguised as yamabushi. As they approached Hiraizumi of Okushū Province they were challenged at Ataka no seki by barrier guards who were on the look out for the party. The leader of the garrison, Togashi Zaemon, deeply suspecting that he had Yoshitsune in his grasp, cross-examined

them. The huge Benkei extracted a scroll of some kind from his pack and read in a forceful manner what he claimed was the *Kanjinchō sūtra* in order to divert the attention of the inquisitors from his master. One of the border guards remarked that the last of the priests (the delicately framed Yoshitsune) looked suspicious, whereupon Benkei lambasted his master, beating him with his staff, and complaining that with such idle fellows in the entourage they should not reach their next destination before nightfall. Togashi Zaemon, alone of the enemy who had realised who the priests really were, offered Benkei wine, impressed by his loyalty to a lost cause, and Yoshitsune was allowed to pass freely.

Konkan was the sixth generation of the Iwamoto school in Edo. His style, which owes much to the Nara school with colourful high-relief inlay, reflects the free and easy nature of the city during the eighteenth century, and usually depicts either human beings or sea creatures.

122

121 Kozuka *(illus. in colour on p. 88)*

Decorated with *sennin* and tiger in
silver, shakudō and gold high-relief
inlay on shakudō nanako ground;
reverse silver with engraved waves

Edo period, 18th century
Signed: Furukawa Mototaka and with maker's
mark
L. 10.4 cm

Mototaka was a pupil of Yokoya Sōmin in
Edo (see p. 116). He inherited his teacher's
skill at both high-relief inlay and also katakiri
bori, yet his work has a unique style in
many ways freer than that of his master.

The *sennin* are Chinese Taoist immortals,
humans who by the practice of austerities
have obtained magical powers.

122 Tsuba

Decorated with Nitta Yoshisada in
gold, shakudō and copper high-relief
inlay on shakudō nanako ground

Edo period, 19th century
Signed: Seishunki. Ōtsuki Seishunki of Kyoto
(d. 1858, aged 54)
H. 8.0 cm

The Minamoto General Nitta Yoshisada,
when serving the Hōjō Shogun, was
persuaded by Prince Morinaga to change
sides to support Emperor Godaigo and
attack Kamakura in 1333. He is shown
receiving the letter which brought about
the change of heart.

123 Tsuba *(illus. in colour on p. 107)*

Shinchū, pierced and carved with mist across the moon

Edo period, 19th century
Signed: Kishōtei Mitsuhiro and with maker's mark.
   Ōtsuki Mitsuhiro (1795–1841)
H.. 7.9 cm

This tsuba shows the crescent moon as the pierced void in the design, with layers of mist drifting across it carved roundly on the solid portions. The subject is appropriate for the school, for *ōtsuki* translates literally as 'large moon'.
   Mitsuhiro specialised in the use of patinated brass and copper like his father Mitsuoki, founder of the Ōtsuki school.

125   *enlarged by 30%*

124   Pair of tsuba for daishō

(illus. in colour on p. 111)

Decorated with nightingales on flowering plum boughs in high-relief coloured-metal inlay on shakudō nanako ground

Edo period, 18th–19th century
Signed: Ishiguro Masatsune (1760–1828) and with
   maker's mark
H. 7.6 and 7.1 cm

Masatsune was taught by Katō Naotsune and his teacher Naomasa of the Yanagawa school, who had been a direct pupil of Yokoya Sōmin (no. 112), the generally accepted innovator of the machibori movement. He specialised in bird and flower designs in high-relief sculpture with coloured-metal inlay, in richness of detail perhaps surpassing the colourful work of the Yokoya group.

125   Tsuba

Decorated with opposed dragons in high relief with gold inlay among waves deeply carved on shakudō nanako ground

Edo period, 19th century
Signed: Tomita Nobukiyo (1817–84) and with
   maker's mark
H. 8.2 cm

Born in Kyoto as Kinoshita Tetsunosuke, Nobukiyo married into the Tomita family who were hereditary Shintō attendants at the Kamo Shrine. He studied metalwork under Gotō Mitsuyasu from the age of fifteen, and at twenty-five became independent and moved to Edo where he eventually became retained by the Nambu clan. He specialised in tsuba with dragons in high-relief inlay like this piece, in line with his upbringing in the Gotō tradition.

126   *enlarged by 30%*

126   Tsuba

Iron, pierced with high-relief
coloured-metal inlay with the theme
Aritōshi Myōjin

19th century
Signed: Seiryoken Katsuhira and with maker's
   mark. Hagitani Katsuhira (1804–86)
H. 8.5 cm

The theme is a story told in the *Ōkagami*
('Great Mirror', *c.* 1100) and also in the
Makura no Sōshi ('The Pillow Book', *c.* 1000)
of a tradition of the shrine named Aritōshi
Myōjin ('The Ant-route Deity') in Nagatake
village of Izumi Province. A Chinese
emperor had posed the difficult problem to
a Japanese emperor of how to pass a thread
through the contorted hole in a bead. An
official solved the puzzle by tying a thread
around the body of an ant and introducing
it into one end of the hole, the other end
having been smeared with honey. The
official became a minister and was
eventually deified as Aritōshi Myōjin.

The tale might well have arisen from
some diplomatic or family incident between
China and Japan before historic records were
kept by the latter. This popular theme has
been represented on screens painted by
Hanabusa Itchō and Sakai Hōitsu, both
artists who worked closely with the
machibori metalworkers.

The design shows a shrine attendant and
refers to a legend that the horse of a
traveller, Ki no Tsurayuki, stopped before
the shrine unable to proceed, until the shrine
attendant told the rider that the presence of
the deity was responsible. Ki no Tsurayuki
recited a poem invoking the deity, and the
horse was able to continue.

The maker of this tsuba, Katsuhira, was
retained as a maker of sword-fittings by the
daimyō of his native Mito Province. Among
his many pupils his third son succeeded to
the name Katsuhira. The work of the school
is predominantly high-relief sculpture of
animals and plants, and often Chinese
figures.

127 Midokoromono

Carved with 'early spring' in high relief with gold inlay on shakudō ground on kozuka and kōgai, and on gold menuki

Signed (all pieces): Kikuoka Mitsuyuki (1750–1800) and with maker's marks
L. (kozuka) 9.7 cm

Straw packages of clams with Nanten (Nandin) and Fukuju sō (Adonis) are auspicious emblems of the New Year. 'Nanten' is a pun since the pronunciation of the word can mean 'to turn away misfortune', and 'Fukuju sō' combines the characters for fortune and longevity.

Mitsuyuki studied under Yanagawa Naomitsu, who had been schooled in the Yokoya tradition. As was the custom in those days, he entered the lay priesthood in his maturity, adopting the name Nansen.

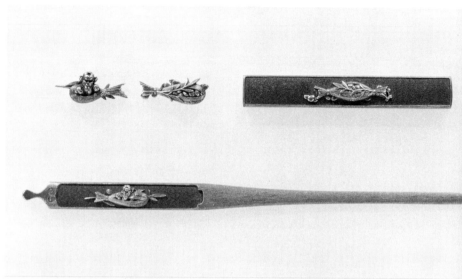

127 *enlarged by 30%*

128 Midokoromono with fuchi/kashira

(illus. in colour on p. 86)

Decorated with eight sennin in high-relief coloured-metal inlay on shakudō nanako and gold ground

Edo period, 19th century
Signed (fuchi): Jūō Hōgen; (kozuka) Ryū Hōgen Kiyotoshi; (kōgai) Toryusai Hōgen; all art names of Tanaka Kiyotoshi (1804–76) together with his Buddhist rank, Hōgen
L. (kozuka) 9.7 cm

Kiyotoshi's version of the group of eight sennin on this matching set of hilt-fittings is a masterpiece of miniature sculpture made in his later years. Kiyotoshi rivals in skill the other great master of the nineteenth century who had also achieved the Buddhist rank Hōgen, Gotō Ichijō.

129 Fuchi/kashira *(illus. in colour on p. 88)*

Decorated with tigers carved in high-relief on shinchū *chiridori ishime* ('plovers stone grain', since surface resembles a great flock of plovers) ground, with gold inlay

Edo period, 18th century
Signed: Yasuchika. Tsuchiya Yasuchika (1670–1744)
L. (fuchi) 3.8 cm; (kashira) 3.6 cm

Yasuchika was one of the most versatile of all the machibori artists, accomplished in varied techniques and familiar with different materials. In his late age he entered the lay priesthood, taking the name Tōu, and passing his name on to Yasuchika II (no. 84).

130 *enlarged by 30%*

131 *enlarged by 30%*

132 *enlarged by 30%*

130 Fuchi/kashira

Carved wuth *kyokusui* party in gold, copper and shakudō high-relief inlay on shakudō nanako ground

Edo period, 19th century
Signed: Oite ('at') Tōfu Sakuragawabe ('Sakuragawabe in the Eastern capital – Edo') saku kore ('this was made'), and Ōto (Imperial capital). Gotō Hokkyō Ichijō (1791–1876)
L. 3.9 cm and 3.1 cm

Kyokusui was an open-air pastime for the literati and nobility. Cups of wine, in this case fixed on the backs of model birds, were floated down a stream. The participants had to compose a poem in the time before the cups reached them, after which they drank the wine. The fuchi is decorated with cockerels by a fence.

Gotō Ichijō, the last active swords-fittings maker of the great family, combined the traditions of the school with a masterly technique and a broad and adventurous range of subject-matter and design. He was highly acclaimed and numbered the Imperial family among his sponsors. The signature on the fuchi of this set contains the word Hokkyō ('Bridge of the Law'), a Buddhist title which he received in 1824, the year he made the fittings for the Emperor Kokaku's sword by Masamune. He progressed to the further rank of Hōgen in 1863, when he was in Kyoto, yet again making a sword mounting, this time for the Emperor Komei.

131 Fuchi/kashira

Carved with daimyō and monkey trainer, in high-relief coloured-metal inlay on shibuichi ground

Edo period, 18th century
Signed: Nagatsune and with maker's mark. Ichinomiya Nagatsune (1721–86)
L. 3.8 cm and 3.3 cm

The theme is one of a number of *kyogen* (comic drama performed in the interval between Nō plays) which make daimyō a subject of fun.

Nagatsune specialised in both high-relief inlay work and katakiri bori engraving. He studied his craft under Yasui Takanaga, from whose name he derived the first character in his own name, and was taught pictorial design by the painter Ishida Yutei.

132 Fuchi/kashira

Carved with Kurama tengu in high-relief coloured-metal inlay on shinchū ground

Edo period, 18th century
Signed: Hakuhotei Iwamoto Konkan (1744–1801) and with maker's mark
L. (fuchi) 3.7cm; (kashira) 3.2 cm

The long-nosed leader of the tengu, creatures who inhabit the Kurama mountains, is shown on the kashira, with two of his beaked and winged companions. Tengu are often depicted, as on this set, in the costume of the yamabushi (devotees of the Shugendō sect, p. 61), who were possibly the origin of these mythical beings.

Konkan was a pupil and adopted son of Ryōkan, the fifth generation of the Iwamoto school. His designs include fish, insects and human figures, usually of popular subjects dear to the hearts of the people of Edo. He was succeeded by the best of several pupils, Konri, who in turn nurtured a flourishing studio in the ninteenth century.

133 *reverse, enlarged by 30%*

133   Tsuba *(illus. in colour on p. 112)*

Iron, carved in high-relief and gold-inlaid details with geese beneath silver-inlaid autumn moon on face and young among waterside grasses on reverse

Edo period, 19th century
Signed: Natsuo sen ('carved by Natsuo) and with inlaid gold seal. Kanō Natsuo (1828–98)
H. 8.4 cm

This tsuba is typical of works by Natsuo showing his affinity with nature and clearly indicates his schooling in the Shijō style of painting.

Kanō Natsuo was born in Kyoto, and at an early stage studied painting under Nakamura Raishō and metalwork under Ikeda Takanobu, from whom he derived his early name, Nobuo. After the Meiji Restoration of 1867 his mastery of realistic pictorial representations was put to use on purely ornamental metalwork such as inlaid plaques and vases. He was at home with both iron and soft metals, and often used the level-inlay technique in conjunction with masterly katakiri bori. Natsuo became Professor of the Tokyo School of Art in 1889 and was invested as an Imperial Craftsman. His many pupils made study pieces based on his work.

134   Menuki *(illus. in colour on p. 112)*

Decorated with sun and moon among waves and clouds in silver and gold high-relief sculpture

Edo period, 19th century
Signed: Kanō Natsuo saku ('made by Kanō Natsuo')
L. 8.3 cm and 8.4 cm

This elegant pair of menuki represent the best of Natsuo's natural style. They were most probably made as part of a rich *en suite* mounting, with the piece bearing the sun on the side of the hilt facing outwards when the sword was worn.

135 Helmet

Edo period, 17th century
H. (overall) 28.2 cm

The style for exotically shaped helmets was
set in the Momoyama period, when a
decorative theme was sometimes expanded
over the whole of a tōsei gusoku. This
helmet, of iron covered in leather and
lacquered black overall, is of the *oki tenugui*
('placed towel') type, which was first
introduced in the form of folded plates of
iron imitating a towel worn tied around the
head. The short multi-purpose tenugui is
worn wrapped around the head to hold the
hair in place and to prevent sweat from
running down into the eyes. Knotted at the
front it signifies festivity; at the back,
business or war.

135

南无阿弥陀佛

136 Helmet

Edo period, 18th century
H. (bowl) 16.9 cm; (overall) 86.3 cm
Kyoto National Museum

The bowl of this helmet is of the Etchū style, composed of a few plates riveted together, high and with rather flat sides. It is striking with its tall lacquered wood *go rin no tō* ('five-tiered tower') Buddhist crest, pierced with a Sanskrit character and bearing in gold lacquer the invocation 'Namu Amida Butsu' ('Hail to Amida Buddha'), and its horned shishi mask with the ears of a more domestic beast where there would in previous ages have been fukigaeshi. There is a mon of the character *tsuchi*, meaning 'ground', on the tower in high relief, and another on the back of the helmet. The shikoro is in five layers of iron wrapped with leather and lacquered overall, linked together with dark blue braid. Documentary evidence suggests that the helmet was commissioned of an armourer of the Iwai family in 1722 by a deeply religious gentleman of the Matsudaira clan.

137 Tōsei gusoku

Dated: In accordance with 1742
Signed (cuirass, in gold): Yukiyasu; (helmet)
    Myōchin Nobuie
H. (cuirass) 54.5 cm
Victoria and Albert Museum, M59–1953

The lacquered iron plate cuirass of this armour is of the type called *yuki no shita* (literally 'beneath the snow'). Its origin lies in the namban pieces developed in the late seventeenth century in response to the promulgation of firearms. Date Masamune, the daimyō of Sendai Province in Northern Japan, adopted the style, and it continued to be worn by his retainers throughout the Edo period.

The armour is of luxurious make with several interesting features. The gourd-shaped metal plates on the chain-mail kote open to reveal a small circular depression, possibly to carry ink or medicine. Unusually, those parts of the kote which cover the wrists and hands are separate, forming gauntlets which attach by buttons on to the ends of the sleeves. The suneate are each composed of three hinged vertical lacquered iron plates in earliest style, like those on Date Masamune's original armour. The eleven sections of the kusazuri, which hang from the bottom of the cuirass, are each composed of five lacquered leather plates, while the haidate is made with gold-lacquered iron plates.

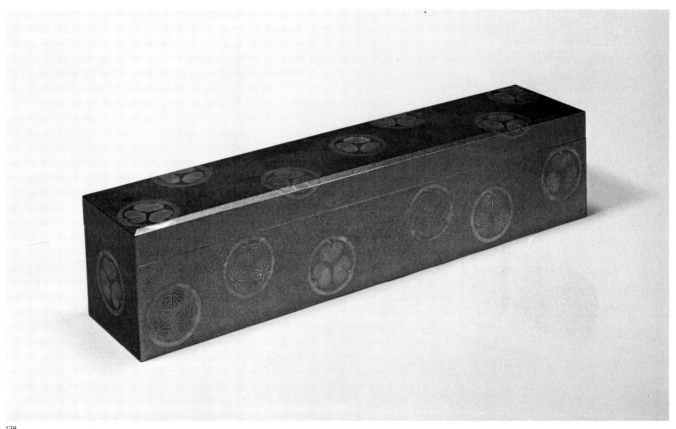

138

138 Box for tantō

Nashiji gold-lacquered with triple hollyhock mon
  of Tokugawa family
Edo period, 17th century
L. 51.0 cm

Lacquered boxes such as this were used by
persons of rank for both storage and
transport of swords, especially when giving
presents. This fine-quality piece is a rare
example from the early Edo period.

139

139 Sword stand

Decorated with peonies and *karakusa*
('Chinese grasses') scrolling in gold
lacquer on black ground

Edo period, 18th century
H. 39.5 cm; W. (at base) 65.0 cm
Sword Museum, Tokyo

Since long swords were carried only out of
doors, stands were often kept just within
the entrances to houses; but they were also
required in the deepest parts of the house,
for the samurai was never without his short
sword and went armed to his bedroom at
night.

This *katana kake*, or sword stand, can hold
three long swords.

140

140 Sword stand

Decorated with clematis and rural hut
among bamboos in gold hiramakie
on black ground

Edo period, 18th century
H. 37.0 cm; w. (at base) 66.0 cm
Sword Museum, Tokyo

This katana kake is for both katana and
wakizashi.

141 Hanging scroll

Ink on paper
Edo period, 19th century
Yamaoka Tesshū (1826–88)
123 × 62.5 cm

Like Miyamoto Musashi some 200 years
previously, Tesshū was a swordsman who
through a lifetime of diligent study of kendō,
Zen and calligraphy had become
enlightened. Originally schooled in the Ono
Ha Ittōryū tradition, he established the
Mutō Ryū, or 'No Sword School'. Although
training in his Mutō Ryū is extraordinarily
severe, Tesshū never killed with the sword.
As a young man he had been greatly
instrumental in the relatively peaceful
handover of government from the
Tokugawa Shogun to the Emperor and the
introduction of a democratic system which
owed much to the West. He had been close
to the last Shogun, Yoshinobu, and after the
Imperial restoration became personal tutor
to the young Emperor Meiji. The
enlightened swordsman prepared for the
instant of death sitting in the posture of
meditation, having gathered some of his
friends for a final farewell. His life still
inspires men who have embarked upon the
twofold path 'Bunbu no Itchi', or 'Brush and
Sword in Accord'. He left many masterpieces
of painting and calligraphy, of which this
rendering of a poem describing an autumn
scene in the mountains exemplifies his
unique and confident style:

A tower outside frost-covered trees,
Mirror clear without one clouded spot,
Unchanging colour of the southern
    mountains,
Chrysanthemum in bloom like the rain.

142

142 Memento mori

Handscroll, ink on paper
Edo period, 19th century
Takahashi Deishū (1835–1903)
32.0 × 65.0 cm

Takahashi Deishū was a trusted retainer of the Tokugawa Shogun during the time of the Meiji Restoration. He is well known as one of the 'Three Shū', together with the two other young samurai statesmen, Yamaoka Tesshū (1826–1888, no. 141) and Katsu Kaishū (1823–99). As a close confidant of Tokugawa Keiki, it is believed that he was largely instrumental in persuading the Shogun to accept the inevitability of the Imperial Restoration,

thereby preventing bloodshed on a massive scale. As a young man of just twenty-two Deishū became a lecturer in the Kōbushō academy of military arts, and at twenty-five he was honoured with the title Ise no Kami in recognition of his position as a swordsman.

This charming little ink painting expresses a sentiment central to the swordsman's quest for enlightenment. The accompanying lines read:

Had I not been born,
I need not die,
But since I've been born to die,
I will.

Bibliography

MATSUŌ FUJISHIRO, *Nippon-Tō Jiten*, 2 vols, Tokyo, 1975

W. H. HAWLEY, *Japanese Swordsmiths*, California, 1966

YUICHI HIROI, *Nippon-Tō no Mikata*, Tokyo, 1971

YUICHI HIROI, *Bizen Kaji*, Nippon Bijutsu Series No. 73, Shibundō, Tokyo, 1972

JUNJI HOMMA, *Masamune Sōshū Den no Nagare*, Nippon Bijutsu Series No. 142, Shibundō, Tokyo, 1978

JUNJI HOMMA, *Showa Dai Meitō Zufu*, Society for the Preservation of Japan Art Swords, Tokyo, 1979

JUNJI HOMMA and MASAKUNI ISHII, *Nippon-Tō Meikan*, Yusankaku, Tokyo, 1975

JUNJI HOMMA and KANZAN SATŌ, *Nippon-Tō Zenshū*, Tokuma Shōten, Tokyo, 1966

H. L. JOLY and H. INADA, *Sword and Samé*, London, 1913

SUSUMU KASHIMA, *Tōsōgu*, Nippon Bijutsu Series No. 64, Shibundō, Tokyo, 1971

NOBUO OGASAWARA, *Japanese Swords*, Hoikusha, Osaka, 1970

NOBUO OGASAWARA, *Tsuba*, Hoikusha, Osaka, 1975

NOBUO OGASAWARA, *Tōken Yamato to Mino*, Nippon Bijutsu Series No. 137, Shibundō, Tokyo, 1977

NOBUO OGASAWARA, *Shintō*, Nippon Bijutsu Series No. 155, Shibundō, Tokyo, 1979

NOBUO OGASAWARA, *Nippon-Tō no Kanshō Kiso Chishiki*, Shibundō, Tokyo, 1988

NOBUO OGASAWARA, *Nippon-Tō no Rekishi to Kanshō*, Kodansha, Tokyo, 1989

MORIHIRO OGAWA, *Nippon-Tō; Art Swords of Japan*, Japan Society, New York, 1976

MORIHIRO OGAWA, *Japanese Swords and Sword Furniture in the Museum of Fine Arts, Boston*, Ōtsuka Kogeisha, Tokyo, 1987

MORIHIRO OGAWA, *Japanese Master Swordsmiths: The Gassan Tradition*, Museum of Fine Arts, Boston, 1989

MOTOHARU ŌZAKI, *Katchū*, Nippon Bijutsu Series No. 24, Shibundō, Tokyo, 1968

B. W. ROBINSON, *The Arts of the Japanese Sword*, Faber and Faber, London, 1961

KANZAN SATŌ, *Nippon-Tō no Kantei Techō*, Society for the Preservation of Japan Art Swords, Tokyo, 1955

KANZAN SATŌ, *Tōken*, Nippon Bijutsu Series No. 6, Shibundō, Tokyo, 1966 (translated into English by Joe Earle as 'The Japanese Sword', Kodansha International, Tokyo, 1983)

KANZAN SATŌ, *Yamashiro Kaji*, Nippon Bijutsu Series No. 107, Shibundō, Tokyo, 1972

KANZAN SATŌ *et al.*, *Nippon-Tō Taikan*, 9 vols, Ōtsuka Kogeisha, Tokyo, 1966

KANZAN SATŌ and HOMATSU WAKAYAMA, *Tōsō Kodōgu Koza*, 8 vols, Yusankaku, Tokyo, 1973

HOMATSU WAKAYAMA, *Kinkō Jiten*, Shimizu Insatsu, Tokyo, 1970

TAKESHI WAKAYAMA, *Tōsō Kinkō Jiten*, Yusankaku, Tokyo, 1972

YOSHINDO YOSHIHARA and LEON and HIROKO KAPP, *The Craft of the Japanese Sword*, Kodansha International, Tokyo, New York, San Francisco, 1987

Figures

BLADE SHAPES

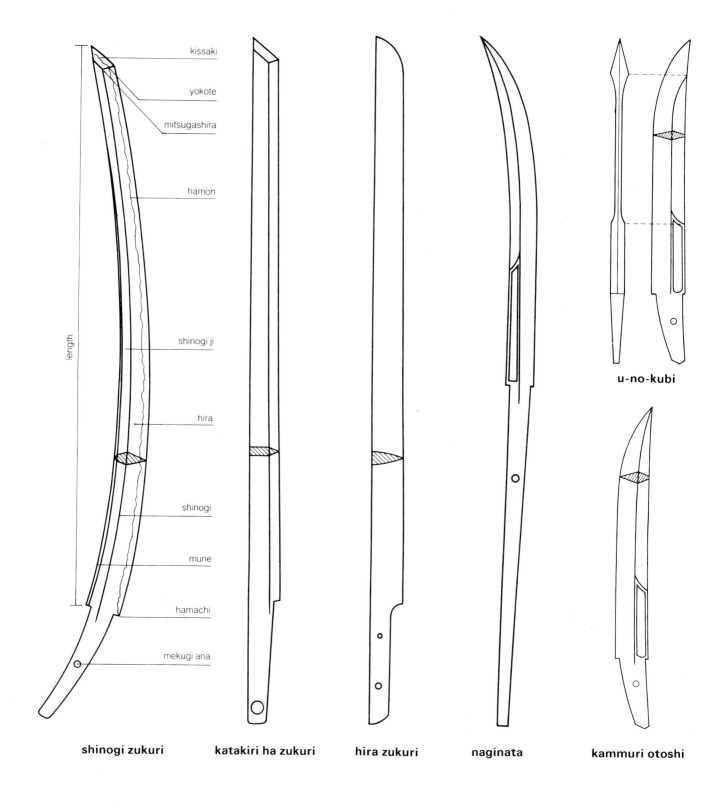

kissaki					
yokote					
mitsugashira					
hamon					
shinogi ji					
hira					
shinogi					
mune					
hamachi					
mekugi ana					

length

u-no-kubi

shinogi zukuri   **katakiri ha zukuri**   **hira zukuri**   **naginata**   **kammuri otoshi**

HADA TYPES

mokume   itame   ayasugi   masame

HAMON STRUCTURES

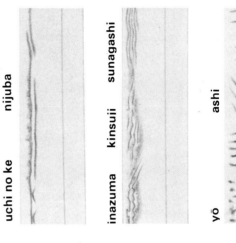

uchi no ke   nijuba   inazuma   kinsuii   sunagashi

yō   ashi

HAMON

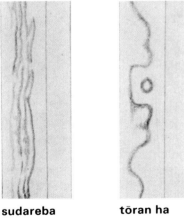

sudareba   tōran ha   hitatsura   notare 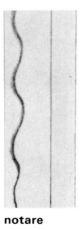   juzuba    sambon sugi

 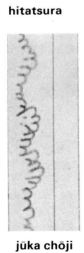   

gunome   kawazu no ko chōji   jūka chōji   chōji   komidare   suguha

Glossary

aikuchi ('meeting mouths'). A type of sword-mounting without a tsuba.

akabe Shoulder-pieces of Kofun period armour which lace together fitting close around the neck.

akoda nari A helmet-bowl shape named after a type of pumpkin, high at the back and slightly swelling forward at the front.

aranie Coarse nie.

ashi ('legs'). Lines falling perpendicularly from the hamon towards the cutting edge.

ashigaru ('light foot') An infantryman, not of samurai class, in the large armies of the Sengoku period.

ayasugi hada ('cryptomeria twill skin'). A sinusoidal grain pattern.

Bakufu The 'Curtain' or 'Camp' Government by samurai.

banzashi ('duty wear'). Another name for the daishō, the matching pair of long and short swords.

bo utsuri ('bar reflection'). A straight form of utsuri found especially on Nambokuchō period swords of the Aoe school and on Ōei era tantō of the Bizen school.

bohi ('bar groove'). A broad groove extending along the shinogi ji of the blade.

boshi ('cap'). That portion of the hamon which turns back to meet the mune at the kissaki section.

bugyō An administrative office.

chikei ('ground shadow'). Bright lines of nie on the ji of the blade.

chirimen, chirimen hada ('silk crepe'). A fine grain with small nie in a complex of round formations resembling silk crepe.

chōji, chōjiba ('cloves'). Hamon pattern resembling a row of packed clove buds.

chokutō A straight-bladed sword of the Kofun and Nara periods.

daienzan ('great circular mountain'). The hemispherical form of Heian and Kamakura period helmet bowls.

daimyō ('great name'). The lord of a province.

daishō ('large and small'). The matching pair of swords worn by the samurai, also known as banzashi.

dōmaru ('trunk wrapping'). A style of armour, strictly the cuirass, which wraps around the body fastening on the right.

dōjō ('place of the Way'). A school for the study of military and other arts with a spiritual basis.

fuchi An oval piece, usually metal, through which the blade passes, and which fits over the end of the hilt next to the tsuba. It frequently matches the kashira in material and decoration.

Fudō Myō-Ō The 'Unmoving', one of the five 'Kings of Light' of esoteric Buddhism.

fukigaeshi ('sweep back'). The turned-back shields forming a continuation of the shikoro at both sides of the front of a helmet.

fukurin A cladding used to cover the rims of tsuba, ridges on helmets and other metallic edges.

fumbari ('bottom' or 'tenacity'). The sudden widening of certain blades at the koshi.

furiko A Shintō wand with several bells attached.

fushi ('thicket'). Thickets in hamon, especially in the straight hamon of certain smiths of the Muromachi period Mino school.

gō ban kaji The smiths who attended the sword-making cloistered Emperor Go Toba in rotation.

gomabashi Carving in the form of two short parallel grooves representing Buddhist ritual tongs.

gunome An abruptly undulating form of hamon.

gyōyō Leaf-shaped plates covering the shoulder-straps at the front of armour other than ōyoroi.

habaki The collar which fits around the blade in front of the tsuba.

hachimanza The decorative surround to the tehen no ana.

hada ('skin'). The surface steel, used to describe the grain of a blade.

hadagane ('skin steel'). The outer layer of steel on a complex blade.

haidate The armoured apron worn under the kusazuri of the cuirass.

hakikake ('swept'). A form of boshi in which the hamon divides into fine lines which sweep up to meet the mune with no return.

hako gunome Hamon with squarish abrupt undulations shaped like boxes.

hamachi The end of the sharp edge, where the blade abruptly narrows into the tang.

hamaguri ba ('clam blade'). A blade whose hira ji is of slightly convex cross-section, found on many blades up until the late Kamakura period.

hamon The crystalline pattern formed along the hardened edge of the blade.

handachi ('half-tachi'). A sword with metal fittings similar to a tachi, but worn through the belt like an uchigatana.

haniwa A pottery model, frequently of animal or of human form, associated with burial in the Kofun period.

happo biraki ('open in all eight directions'). A kendō attitude without set form.

happuri An iron protection for the forehead and cheeks in popular use up to the Muromachi period.

hara ate A breast plate covering only the front of the body, worn by ashigaru during the Muromachi period, from which the present-day kendō body armour developed.

haramaki A form of armour, strictly a cuirass, which wraps around the trunk and joins down the back.

Heianjō sukashi School of pierced-iron tsuba-makers, generally earlier than Kyō sukashi.

hi A groove carved along the length of a sword.

hijiki hada A jihada with thick bands of jinie, named after hijiki, a kind of edible seaweed. *See also* matsukawa.

hira The 'flat' of a blade, i.e. the sides which meet to form the cutting edge.

hira ji ('flat ground'). The ground of the flat surfaces which meet to form the cutting edge of a blade.

hira tachi A tachi whose scabbard is of rather flat section, common during the Heian period, and reflecting the early blade shape.

hira zogan Inlay work level with the surface of the ground of sword-fittings.

hira zukuri ('flat make'). Type of blade of triangular cross-section having no shinogi.

hitatsura A structure of similar consistency to the hamon formed throughout the surface of the blade.

hitsuana The holes pierced through the tsuba to accommodate the blade and the passage of the kozuka and kōgai.

hiza yoroi Knee armour of the Kofun period.

hoate An iron mask for the lower part of the face.

Hōgen 'The Eye of the Law' – a Buddhist title.

Hokkyō 'The Bridge of the Law' – a Buddhist rank.

hoko A short-bladed polearm of the Kofun and Nara periods.

hōkyū The 'treasure jewel' of Buddhist understanding.

horimono Decorative, structural, or religious carving on the blade of a sword.

hoshi kabuto ('star helmet'). Helmet formed of vertical curved plates fixed together with rivets, or 'stars', which project outwards in regular rows.

hotsure ('fraying'). Lines of nie straying away from the hamon above and below resembling frayed thread.

hyōgo kusari tachi Military tachi of the late Heian and Kamakura periods suspended by chains from the belt, frequently dedicated to temples and shrines.

hyōtan ba A hamon used by the swordsmith Nagasone Kotetsu which is reminiscent of the shape of the hyōtan, a double gourd.

ichimai boshi ('single-sheet cap'). A boshi which fills the whole of the kissaki portion of the blade.

iebori ('house carvers'). Metal sword-fittings makers in the service of the Shogun during the Muromachi and Edo periods.

ikakeji An unburnished lacquer surface sprinkled overall, usually with gold particles.

ikubi kissaki ('bull neck point'). A stubby kissaki found on broad-bladed work of the middle Kamakura period, and often on later blades made for dedication to temples and shrines.

inazuma ('lightening'). Lines of nie through and around the hamon.

inrō kizami Ribbed carving on scabbards and shafts resembling the shape of some inrō (medicine or seal containers).

ishime The hammered stone-ground effect on metal sword-fittings.

ishizuki The chape on a tachi scabbard.

itame 'Wood-plank grain' on a sword blade.

ito maki no tachi A tachi mounting bound with braid on both the hilt and the upper part of the scabbard to prevent abrasion of the lacquer against armour.

ji ('ground') – shinogi ji being the parallel surfaces of the shinogi region, and hira ji being the surfaces which meet at an angle forming the cutting edge.

jifu ('ground spots'). Patches of nie on the ji.

jigane ('ground steel'). The grain or, strictly speaking, the steel surface of the ji.

jihada ('ground skin'). *See* jigane.

jimbaori An armour surcoat.

jingasa The shallow conical hard hat worn by ashigaru in the Muromachi period, and later by samurai on official duty during the Edo period.

jinie Nie on the ji of the blade.

jujitsu ('fullness'). Complete understanding, or selflessness, in Zen.

jūka chōji ('banked' chōji). A broad hamon with densely packed banks of chōji.

jūmonji yari A type of yari with two blades transverse to the central blade in the form of a cross.

juzuba A hamon in the form of the row of beads of a rosary.

kabukimono Society of rōnin during the early Edo period.

kabuto gane ('helmet metal'). The kashira on a tachi mounting.

kabutsuchi gata tachi Mounting for a chokutō of the Kofun period with a large bulbous pommel.

kaeri tsuno ('return horn'). A horn-shaped projection below the kurikata on an uchigatana mounting which prevents the scabbard from slipping upwards.

kage sukashi ('shadow piercing). Pierced sculpture in negative silhouette.

kakinagashi Manner in which grooves in a blade continue through the tang.

kami The gods of the Shintō religion.

kammuri otoshi ('crown drop'). A type of dagger blade shape with a double-return edge, and a distinctively shaped shinogi ji.

kanagushi General term for metal-fittings maker.

kane ('steel'). Used when speaking of jihada or jigane.

kani no tsume ('crab's claws'). A hamon in which the heads of the gunome break into pincer-like formations.

kanteishō A document of appraisal.

kantō tachi Tachi of the Yayoi and Kofun periods with an annular pommel.

kashira The pommel of a sword hilt, usually metal or horn.

kata yoroi Shoulder armour of the Kofun period.

katakama yari A type of yari with either a single-curved transverse blade, or with one of two transverse blades longer than the other.

katakiri bori Method of decorative carving by means of a chisel held at an oblique angle so as to vary the section and depth of the cut in simulation of brush painting.

katakiri ha Blade shape perfectly flat on one side, and with a wide shinogi ji on the other from which the hira ji slopes down abruptly forming the cutting edge.

katana (literally 'sword'). Usually applies to the uchigatana, the longer of the two swords carried by the samurai.

kawazu no ko chōji ('tadpole chōji'). A hamon with high round-ended chōji resembling the heads of tadpoles.

kazari byō Decorative pin or rivet heads.

kazari tachi A decorative tachi mounting used at court from the Nara period until recent times.

kazu uchi mono ('things made in number'). Poor-quality swords made in large numbers during the Muromachi period.

keiko An armour of the Kofun and Nara periods composed of linked iron plates.

keitō gata tachi ('jewel-head type tachi'). Mounting for a chokutō of the Kofun period with a pommel in the form of a Chinese jade jewel.

ken A straight double-edged blade, primarily made for esoteric Buddhist ritual.

kendō ('the Way of the Sword'). The spiritual study of swordplay.

kensaku The rope or lassoo attribute of Fudō Myō-Ō and other Buddhist deities.

kenuki gata tachi ('tweezer-shaped sword'). A form of tachi of the Heian period whose tang forms the hilt and which is pierced with a longitudinal hole resembling a pair of tweezers.

kesa giri ('surplice cut'). A sword-cut diagonally down through one shoulder and out on the opposite side of the trunk.

kijimata ('pheasant's thigh'). The tang shape of certain Heian and Kamakura period tachi.

kiku gō saku ('noble chrysanthemum make'). Swords marked on the tang with the Imperial chrysanthemum and made in the forge of the cloistered Emperor Go Toba in the early Kamakura period.

kikusui ('chrysanthemum and water'). A hamon in the form of chrysanthemum blossoms floating on a stream.

kinsuji Usually applied to lines of nie similar to, yet shorter than, inazuma in the hamon.

kinza The gold mint.

kissaki The point section of the blade.

kobushi gata chōji ('fist-shaped chōji'). A hamon devised by Kawachi no Kami Kunisuke.

kōgai A kind of bodkin carried in a pocket at the side of the scabbard.

koitame Small itame grain.

kojiri The chape of a scabbard.

komaru A small round return of the boshi.

kondei ('stalwart youth'). System introduced in AD 762 whereby noble families sent their sons as cadets in the standing army.

kongōtai The 'diamond', or ultimately real world, as opposed to the illusory world of human understanding.

konie Small or fine nie.

konuka hada ('rice flour' hada). A fine form of itame grain found on swords of Hizen Province during the Edo period, named after the rice flour which ladies used as a facial cosmetic.

koshi ('waist'). The 'waist' or lower portion of a blade just above the hilt.

koshi zori ('waist curve'). A curve which distinctly deepens at the koshi of the sword, found on most swords of the late Heian to middle Kamakura periods, some Muromachi period swords and some shinshintō blades.

koshigatana ('waist sword'). An early term for a short sword or dagger.

koshihi ('waist groove'). A short groove carved along the shinogi ji near the 'waist' or bottom part of the blade just above the hilt.

koshimono ('waist thing'). A sword worn at the belt.

kote The sleeves and integral gauntlets of an armour.

kotō ('old swords'). Swords made before the Keichō era, as opposed to shintō, made after then.

kozane The small plates of lacquered iron or leather which are linked together to form items of armour.

kozuka ('small hilt'). The rectangular hilt of the small knife kept in a pocket at the side of the scabbard.

kuchi kanamono ('mouth metal piece'). The collar fitting at the mouth of a tachi scabbard.

kurikara Buddhist emblem in the form of a dragon coiled around a vajra-hilted ken-type sword carved on the blade.

kurikata ('chestnut shape'). The small protrusion on the side of uchigatana mountings pierced with a hole to take the sageo cord.

kusazuri The skirt of an armour formed of linked kozane and suspended from the cuirass.

kuwagata ('hoe shape'). The horn-like crests often mounted at the front of the helmet, and also a horimono on sword blades.

Kyō sukashi A school of pierced-iron tsuba-makers associated with Kyoto during the Momoyama and Edo periods.

kyubi no ita A loose hanging plate over the left breast of the oyoroi.

mabishi tsuki kabuto Helmet with a peak.

machibori ('town carvers'). The studios of decorative sword-fittings makers which became established around the end of the seventeenth century in the towns independent of the iebori tradition.

makie ('sprinkled illustration'). A method of decoration by sprinkling gold or other metallic dust on to lacquer before it sets hard.

makikake Method of cross-binding hilts with braid.

martensite The hardest structure in quench-hardened steel, formed of an iron super-saturated with carbon.

maru ('round'). To describe the shape of the boshi.

masame A parallel longitudinal grain.

matsukawa ('pine skin'). A distinctive hada similar to hijiki hada to describe the work of the Nambokuchō period smith Norishige of Etchū and others.

mekiki A connoisseur and appraiser of swords.

mekugi The peg which passes through the hilt and a hole (mekugi ana) in the tang to secure the blade in the hilt.

menoko A type of Nara period Chinese-style armour made of small iron plates mounted on a textile coat.

menuki Ornamental metal pieces positioned either side of the hilt.

mete zashi ('horse-hand sword'). A dagger worn at the right side of the waist with the cutting edge forward, and used to cut upwards under the armour.

midare komi A boshi which undulates away from the edge.

midareba A hamon of wild or uncontrolled form.

midokoromono ('things of three places'). A matching set of kōgai, kozuka and menuki.

mitsugashira The point where the yokote meets the shinogi.

mokko A quatrefoil tsuba shape.

mokume ('wood grain'). A grain formed of masses of concentric loops.

mon The badge of a family, used on clothing, arms, furniture and various accessories.

monouchi ('hitting part'). That part of the cutting edge of a long sword, about one-quarter down from the kissaki of an uchigatana, which is regarded as the most efficient place to cut.

moroha A double-edged blade.

munaita The metal piece fixed across the front of the ōyoroi at the top to provide reinforcement at the upper chest.

mune The back of the blade.

musōtō ('undecorated sword'). A type of blade made in the Nara period whose tang was made in the form of a hilt to be simply bound with rattan for use.

nagamaki A long-bladed single-edged pole-arm.

naginata A glaive-like pole-arm with a single-edged blade which swells and curves deeply towards the point.

namako ('sea cucumber'). A device used on tsuba by Miyamoto Musashi.

namazu hada ('catfish hada'). Dark splashes of nie on the hira ji, a distinctive form of jifu.

nanako ('fish roe'). The effect on metalwork produced by a hollow-ended punch.

nashiji ('pear skin'). A grain of close-packed mokume.

nie ('boiling'). A metallurgical structure on a blade whose crystals are individually visible with the naked eye, traditionally described as having the appearance of frost on grass, or a cluster of stars on a clear night.

nijuba ('double hamon'). A hamon, usually suguha, forming a double line.

nioi ('visual fragrance'). A metallurgical structure whose crystals are not individually discernible with the naked eye, visible as a white line which is traditionally likened to the appearance of the Milky Way.

nodachi ('moor sword'). A very long sword favoured during the Nambokuchō period, also known as a seoi dachi.

nodowa A gorget.

notare ('undulating'). Applied to hamon.

Nyūdō An appellation indicating one who has entered the path of Buddhist study.

ō sode The large rectangular shields tied at the shoulders of the ōyoroi and sometimes lighter forms of armour.

ōitame Large itame grain.

oroshi mune A blade cross-section which narrows from the shinogi towards the mune, developed during the Muromachi period.

oshigata A drawing of a blade showing details of the metallurgy and inscriptions on the tang.

ōyoroi ('great harness'). A heavy armour of the Heian to Nambokuchō periods made for the mounted archer.

pearlite A eutectic mixture of ferrite and cementite with 0.87 per cent carbon.

rendai The Buddhist lotus throne, used in stylised form as a horimono.

rōnin ('wave man'). A masterless samurai.

sageo A braided cord used to tie the uchigatana in place at the belt.

saiba (*saiha*). A blade which has been rehardened by heat treatment some time after its original manufacture due to having lost its temper in a fire, or through having been severely reshaped.

saihai A signalling device and symbol of military rank, formed of animal hair or strips of paper or leather mounted at the end of a baton.

saka chōji ('reverse chōji'). A sloping chōji hamon.

saki zori A curve which deepens in the upper part of the blade, developed during the Muromachi period.

sambon sugi ('three cryptomerias'). A hamon resembling a row of groups of three cryptomeria treetops.

sansaku boshi A boshi which undulates in a gentle inwards depression, and mark of the sansaku ('the three makers') of the Kamakura period Osafune school of Bizen – Nagamitsu, Mitsutada and Sanenaga.

sashimono ('inserted thing'). A flag which can be fixed on to the back of an armour to project above the head.

satetsu ('sand iron'). An iron ore.

seita The plate covering the gap down the back of a haramaki introduced during the Muromachi period.

semegane Reinforcing metal bands on a tachi scabbard.

sendan no ita A loose hanging plate over the right breast of the ōyoroi.

seoi dachi ('sword carried on the back'). Otherwise called nodachi, the very long swords of the Nambokuchō period.

seppa Oval copper spacers fitted either side of the tsuba.

seppa dai The oval centre part of a tsuba through which is pierced the hole for the blade, and against which the two oval seppa spacers fit.

shakudō An alloy of copper with a few per cent of gold and traces of other elements found in the unrefined form of copper called yamagane, which can be patinated to a range of lustrous blacks and purple-blacks.

shibuichi ('one part in four'). An alloy used by the machibori artists composed of one-fourth part silver in copper which could be patinated to a range of colours from silver, through grey, to a variety of browns.

shikoro The hanging neck-guard around the back and sides of a helmet.

shimpu The 'divine wind', also read kamikaze, which wrecked the invasion fleet of the Mongols in 1274, and again in 1281.

shinchū A form of brass.

shingane ('heart steel'). The central core of resilient steel in a blade.

shinogi The longitudinal line dividing the parallel-sided portion (shinogi ji) of the blade from the hira ji.

shinshintō ('new, new swords'). Swords of the late Edo period made in conscious revival of early styles.

shintai A holy object representing the physical manifestation of the deity of a Shintō shrine.

shintō ('new swords'). Swords made after the Muromachi period, by convention after the first year of the Keichō era, 1596, as opposed to kotō made up until then.

Shintō The indigenous religion of deities of nature and creation.

shirake ('white shadow'). A white cloudy mark along the blade resembling utsuri but not controlled. Found on many early blades of the Kyūshū schools and on Seki blades of the Muromachi period.

shishiai bori Carving in sunken relief.

shokaku tsuki kabuto ('battering ram helmet'). A type of helmet of the Kofun period with a pronounced pointed front.

Shugendō The 'mountain religion' containing elements from Buddhism and Shintō and numbering many swordsmiths among its adherents during the kotō era.

soehi ('accompanying groove'). A narrow groove carved immediately under a bohi along the length of a sword.

sōhei Buddhist warrior monks.

sokutō ('bundled swords'). Mass-produced blades made during the Sengoku period, also called kazu uchi mono.

sudareba A form of layered hamon resembling a sudare, or hanging screen of horizontal bamboo strips.

Sue ('end' or 'late'). Late as applied to the later generations of a swordmaking tradition.

suemon zogan A method of pinning sculpted pieces on to the ground of sword-fittings.

suguha A straight hamon.

suibokuga Ink paintings.

suji kabuto ('ridged helmet'). A type of helmet whose bowl is constructed of curved plates joined together and turned up along one edge to form vertical ridges.

suken The 'simple sword' motif used in horimono.

suki A kendō term signifying a gap in awareness.

sukidashi bori ('scooping out carving'). Carving by cutting the ground away to leave the design modelled on the remaining high parts.

sumi hada ('charcoal hada'). A form of jifu.

sunagashi ('drifting sand'). Lines of nie crystals forming thick longitudinal lines within the hamon.

suneate Armour for the lower legs.

suriage The practice of cutting down very long swords to a more convenient length for carrying at the belt.

tachi A general term for a long sword, but specifically for swords made to be mounted suspended loosely from the belt with the cutting edge downwards.

Tanabata A festival on 7 July fêting the two stars 'the herdsman and the weaver girl'.

tanko A form of Kofun period armour composed of broad iron plates tied or riveted together to form a rigid cuirass.

tantō ('short sword'). A dagger.

taori A Nara period word for the sleeves and gauntlets of an armour. *See also* kote.

tawara byō The characteristic tawara ('rice bale') shape of the heads of pins used to fix the tang into the hilt on Heian period and some later tachi.

tehen no ana The hole in the crown of a helmet bowl.

tekkotsu ('iron bones'). The grain in tsuba of the Owari school arising from the hammered preparation of the iron plate.

temari See taori, kote.

tōran ha A 'billowing' hamon.

torii The symbolic gateway on the approach to a Shintō shrine.

tōsei gusoku ('equipment of the times'). A form of armour developed in the late Muromachi period which covered most of the body.

tōsu Small knives with slender blades from a few centimetres up to around ten centimetres long, carried by the nobility during the Nara period.

tsuba The guard of a sword.

tsuba katana General name used in the Edo period for those short swords with a tsuba, also known as chisa katana, which had previously been known as koshigatana.

tsuji giri The illicit practice of cutting down passers-by at crossroads which prevailed during the early seventeenth century.

tsurubashiri ('bowstring run'). The leather covering over the front of the ōyoroi which allows unimpeded passage of the bow string.

u-no-kubi ('cormorant's neck'). A dagger shape similar to kammuri otoshi.

uchi no ke Small upward-pointing crescent-shaped structures along the hamon.

uchi zori ('inner curve'). A slight downward curve in a blade, found mainly on daggers of the middle Kamakura period.

uchigatana ('hitting sword'). A sword meant for making strong downward cuts on foot, as opposed to the wheeling cuts of the cavalryman's tachi.

ude nuke ana Two holes pierced through a tsuba to carry a cord which retains the blade in the scabbard.

uma no ha gunome ('horse-tooth gunome'). A form of abruptly undulating hamon resembling a row of horse's teeth, also called hako gunome.

utsuri ('reflection'). A distinct white shadow along the ji, sometimes of a regular wavy continuous form like a reflection of the hamon.

vajra The pronged implement of esoteric Buddhism representing aspects of Buddhist law.

waidate The side-piece covering the joint on the right of the ōyoroi cuirass.

wakizashi ('side' or 'companion sword'). The shorter of the daishō pair of swords.

warabite tachi ('young fern sword'). A type of Nara period sword with the tang drawn out and turned over in a shape reminiscent of the curled shoot of the fern.

yaguragane The triangular metal pieces to which the suspending cords of a tachi are fitted.

yakidashi That part of the lower end of the hamon on certain blades, mostly of the Edo period, which slopes gently down to the edge in a characteristic form.

yakiire The operation of quenching a heated blade in water to harden the edge, producing the hamon.

yakitsume A boshi in which the hamon ends at the mune without turning back.

yamabushi An adherent of the Shugendō sect.

yamagane ('mountain metal'). A crude copper containing small amounts of impurities which are responsible both for the characteristic patina which develops on yamagane and the alloy shakudō.

yari A pike or spear, used to cut and thrust but never thrown.

yō ('leaves'). Discrete patches within the hamon, similar to ashi but separate from the line of the hamon.

yō sukashi Pierced work in positive silhouette.

yokote The line perpendicular to the mune defining the boundary of the hira ji and the triangular kissaki sections.

yoroi doshi ('armour piercer'). A thick-bladed hira zukuri dagger.

yoroi soroe A complete set of armour including the yoroi, which strictly means the cuirass.

zukuri ('make' or 'form'). For example, shinogi zukuri – a blade having a shinogi.

Index of makers